The Uses of Structuralism

The Uses of Structuralism

by
Raymond Boudon

translated by
Michalina Vaughan

introduced by
Donald MacRae

 HEINEMANN · LONDON

Heinemann Educational Books Ltd
LONDON EDINBURGH MELBOURNE TORONTO
AUCKLAND SINGAPORE JOHANNESBURG
HONG KONG NAIROBI IBADAN NEW DELHI

Cased ISBN 0 435 82155 5
Paper ISBN 0 435 82156 3

Published by Heinemann Educational Books Ltd
48 Charles Street, London W1X 8AH
Printed in Great Britain by
Richard Clay (The Chaucer Press) Ltd
Bungay, Suffolk

Contents

Introduction *by Professor Donald MacRae*   vii

1. *The Term Structure and its Polysemic Character*   I
   The need to give up inductive definitions of the concept
     of structure   3
   The irrelevance of inductive definitions   8
   The criteria of a non-inductive definition of the concept
     of structure   I I
   The concept of system   I3

2. *Two Types of Context of the Concept of Structure;*   I6
   Intentional Definitions
   Two types of context and the distinction between them   I7
   Further examples of the concept of structure in the
     context of an intentional definition   29
   The role of the concept of structure in the context of
     intentional definitions   39
   The meaning of the concept of structure in the context
     of intentional definitions   44
   From the first to the second type of context   48

v

3. *The Meaning of the Concept of Structure in the Context of*   52
   Operative Definitions
   The sources of homonymy in the context of operative
   definitions   56
   The first source of homonymy   58
   The second source of homonymy   60
   First example of type 1   64
   Provisional definition of the concept of structure in
   the context of an operative definition   76
   Second example of type 1   79
   An example of type 2   90
   Conclusion   98

4. *The Concept of Structure in the Context of Operative*
   Definitions: Structures without Apparent Axioms   103
   An example of type 3   103
   Examples of type 4   115
   The concept of verification   122
   Social structure and institutional coherence   126

Conclusion   134

Notes   143

Bibliography   151

Name Index   155

Subject Index   157

Introduction

RAYMOND BOUDON is too little known to writers in the English-speaking countries. In his work he combines an originality of approach and idea, intellectual subtlety and statistical competence. Such a combination is very rare. The present book is essentially analytic and expository. It would be quite false to pretend that it is easy, but it would be equally false to claim that it will not yield to attentive reading by a sympathetic reader. Put differently, it is as easy as its subject-matter permits. No other book so far as I know gives so penetrating and critical an account of the modern uses of the concept of structure and the structural as they are used in linguistics, psychology, anthropology and sociology, or of the logic of their use. It is only to be regretted that the author has not gone further and considered the concepts of structuralism in aesthetic criticism, particularly the criticism of literature. But he has the right, I suggest, to feel that he has done enough. Agree or not, linguistics and social scientists, not to mention philosophers and methodologists will find help and richness here.

So far the English reader has had little aid with this fashionable and, more important, fruitful and exciting area. A few hermetic texts have been made available in rather more hermetic translations. Only, not always well-translated, the works of Claude Lévi-Strauss have been easily accessible of the total of important publication that may be called structuralist. In addition of course, structural linguistics, largely an American enterprise, has been sufficiently known. It must be said, that two admirable expository works were published in London in 1970 introducing the anthropology of Lévi-Strauss and the linguistics of Chomsky.* Yet, as the reader of Boudon will see these are but two provinces, admittedly important, of a much larger realm. What is more the territory of structuralism is open to more and other questions as to the legitimacy of its occupation and boundaries than most people have realized or than are raised by Chomsky and Lévi-Strauss. It is these questions, operative at a high level—as opposed to the deep levels which structuralism claims to reveal—with which Boudon concerns us. The air may be hard to breathe at such heights, but it is invigorating and salutory.

In structuralism are we deceived by a mere clang, a mere assuming of significant identities because the word structure is employed in what are, after all, very different contexts? I suggest that here the reader might do well to begin with Boudon's *Conclusion*, then read the text from the start including once again that conclusion. I think he will decide that we are in fact involved partly in a false sense of unity because of mere association, mere clang, but partly in a genuine process of discovery of underlying structure—the word is unavoidable! Yet if he is familiar with the British tradition in sociology, with Spencer, Hobhouse and Ginsberg, and the British tradition in social anthropology from Spencer through Radcliffe-Brown and Evans-Pritchard†, he may feel a certain worry: in this tradition, rich in achievement, is not structure after all a central concept? Certainly, but is it structuralist? Now some of this tradition, notably some early papers‡ by Evans-Pritchard and perhaps also his later monographic works could, though with violence, be translated into structuralist terms. Nevertheless I feel that here we really will be deceived by the use of similar words for very different things. Which is not to deny the British usage, with its seed-time earlier than Spencer and deep in the Scottish enlightenment, its huge merit and legitimacy. All I am saying is that with this tradition, this usage, Boudon has little to do.

This, however, is not to deny the correctness of his concern with Talcott Parsons and other American or Americanized

* Edmund Leach, *Lévi-Strauss* and John Lyons, *Chomsky*, London and New York 1970.

† The omission of Malinowsky is deliberate.

‡ Especially those on Pareto and on the morphology of magic.

social scientists. Yet on reflection one may find his text both in-conclusive (I think rightly) and his employment of American social scientists more illustrative than probative. Yet, after all, Boudon is not essentially attempting to be probative but to be critical, exegetical and, in the proper sense of the term, prag-matic. In this difficult task I believe he succeeds.

What is obvious here, as elsewhere in Boudon's work is that he is one of the most distinguished and freshly creative of the followers of the greatest of sociologists, Émile Durkheim. The reader indeed may wish that he had more of Boudon himself here, and one may hope that further translations will gratify this wish. But by concentrating on and adding to a neglected side of Durkheim it is clear that Boudon is greatly advancing the human sciences from the doldrums into which they drifted in the 1960s. Perhaps much of the vogue of structuralism has in fact been in its similar promise of movement out of a becalming sea. At a superficial but not negligible level one may say indeed that the central structuralist positions are (1) appearance in human conduct and affairs is not reality, (2) reality is struc-tured, and (3) this structuring is code-like. In a way is that not also a lesson of Durkheim's? I think so, particularly of *The Elementary Forms of the Religious Life*. But it is not the only one, if only because in Durkheim appearance is not just a clue to social reality, but has its own claims in the elaboration of sociological understanding. To pursue this point, however, would take one rather far from the present book.

One last word about it. I have suggested that this is in many ways an austere work. A first reading may gain from an omis-sion of pages 24–7, except perhaps for psychologists with certain precise interests. I do not think that the reader will find this procedure frustrating, and if he does the remedy is in his own hands. What I am sure is that social scientists, scholars, philo-sophers and advanced undergraduate students will gain enor-mously from this text. I already know from personal experience in the supervision of research students how valuable and stimulating this book can be.

DONALD G. MACRAE
Highgate, January 1971

The Uses of Structuralism

1

The Term Structure and its Polysemic Character

AMONG the key concepts in the human sciences, that of structure is undoubtedly one of the most obscure, as is shown by the number of works and the amount of discussion devoted to it in the last ten years.[1] If this concept were less ambiguous, obviously fewer efforts would be required to define it. Quite apart from the multiplicity of definitions, the use of the actual word 'structure', at least in certain contexts, gives rise in itself to considerable dissatisfaction. The variety of connotations characterizing the term when employed by different authors raises doubts as to the existence of a single meaning which could be attributed to it, or of a single method—or at least a single methodological orientation—which could be termed 'structuralist'. It raises the question whether the outstanding contributions of certain 'structuralists' are not 'the product of their genius rather than the outcome of their method', as Leibnitz said of Descartes' analytical geometry.

These difficulties are acknowledged by the majority of authors who have attempted, individually or collectively, to analyse the concept of structure. On the one hand, there is a universal recognition among them of the fundamental importance of this concept for the human sciences. On the other, they cannot fail to recognize the ambiguity surrounding it. Inescapably, the coexistence of these two positions leads to uneasiness, since it is difficult to assert the merits of a concept or a methodology while at the same time admitting that its nature is, to say the least, unclear.

Difficulties are increased when to the initial ambiguity of the concept one must also add the uncertainty resulting from its association with a number of other concepts, by reference to which it is generally defined. The concepts usually associated with structure are 'system', 'coherence', 'whole', 'dependence of the parts on the whole', 'set of relationships', 'whole irreducible to the sum of its parts', etc.

In view of this, can such difficulties not be overcome by defining the concept of structure in the light of those concepts associated with it which have the advantage of being unanimously accepted? This is the approach adopted by Piaget [48] when he states that: 'A structure (in the most general sense) exists when elements are united in a whole which presents certain properties as a whole and the properties of the elements are wholly or partially dependent on those of the whole' (p. 34). Another example of defining structure by reference to concepts associated with it is provided by Flament [15]: 'A structure is a sum of elements related to one another, such that any modification in one element or in one relationship entails a modification in other elements or relationships' (p. 417).

Piaget's definition seems to have struck even its author as unsatisfactory, since several years later [49] he admitted that defining the concept of structure raises 'somewhat frightening problems' and that the meaning of this term 'usually remains imprecise' (p. 7). The significance of this statement is enhanced by the world-wide repute of Piaget's contribution to the analysis of psychological structures.

Nevertheless the two definitions quoted may, when considered at face value, be regarded as equivalent. They differ only in nuance and are both founded on an assimilation of the concept of structure to its associations. In addition, without citing further examples, it could be asserted that the majority of current definitions available for the concept of structure would be comparable with these.

The difficulty is thus not one of formulating a universally acceptable definition. It is rather that a definition of this kind outlines a concept so crude and banal as to be inadequate to account for the scientific impact of structural anthropology or structural linguistics. Moreover if the concept of structure could be defined by reference to synonyms such as 'system of relationships', 'sum of elements being greater than its parts', etc., why should a more ambiguous term be used? More importantly, how does one explain the fact that on linguistic and epistemological grounds the use of this term should appear indispensable not only to the linguistician and the anthropologist, but also to the sociologist, psychologist or economist?

The need to give up inductive definitions of the concept of structure

It is hoped to show that the difficulties and contradictions outlined can be resolved by a change in methodological perspective. The need for such a change was stated by Lévi-Strauss [30]: '. . . the concept of structure is not amenable to an inductive definition, based on a comparison of and abstraction from the common elements characterizing all meanings of the term as generally used. Either the term social structure has no meaning or this meaning itself already has a structure. It is the latter concept of structure which must be grasped first . . .' (p. 305).

It seems evident that the concept of structure cannot be inductively defined, in the sense given by Lévi-Strauss to such a definition. When a concept has its support in objective reality, as for example 'dog', a concept dear to Kant, it is possible to attempt its definition by comparing and abstracting the elements common to those objects which it designates. In our example, the concept of dog would be defined by comparing and abstracting the elements common to all individual dogs. But what of the concept of 'structure'? Clearly, comparing and abstracting would take place on the level of secondary sources and could not use any other material than the definitions of the concept of structure propounded by different authors in different disciplines. While dogs exist and have a reality independent from the definitions which could be given to the concept of dog, this does not hold for 'structures', which do not exist until they have been defined. An analysis of definitions given to the notion of structure by economists, sociologists or psychologists provides information on the definitions themselves, but does not produce, through comparing and abstracting their common elements, a definition of *the* concept of structure. The common elements of these definitions are not so difficult to trace: these are the associations and negative associations referred to earlier. Thus it seems certain that the classical definitional techniques, founded on *genus proxim* and *differentia specifica*, or more generally inductive definitions in Lévi-Strauss's sense, will necessarily be of little help in discovering the meaning of the concept of structure.

While the inadequacy of an inductive definition is perfectly clear, the same cannot be said for the statement made by Lévi-Strauss that: 'Either the term social structure has no meaning or this meaning itself already has a structure'. What is meant by the structure of the meaning of the term structure?

This lofty formulation may be better understood if it is remembered that, on the one hand, Lévi-Strauss publicly acknowledges his debt to structural phonology and, on the other, that the fundamental problem of phonology—at least until recent times—has precisely been to seek *a* definition of the phonemes of a language. Thus phonology offers a theory of defining, and it is this theory that Lévi-Strauss seeks to apply to the concept of structure.

Taking as an example the sound which is transcribed in French by the symbol *r*, we are all aware that this sound has an identity. However if one tries to describe this entity inductively, in the tradition of classical phonetics, by expressing the elements common to possible pronunciations of the sound *r*, one immediately meets the difficulty which phonetics has never surmounted. The pronunciation of this sound varies considerably from one individual to another, and the same individual may produce it differently according to context. Yet everyday experience confirms that a meaningful series of sounds is correctly identified even if the pronunciation is extremely defective. Therefore there is an entity, (*r*), which cannot be reduced without arbitrariness to a sum of common elements—due to diversity in its pronunciation—but its identity is nevertheless clear. In other words, any *inductive* definition of (*r*) fails to account for the identity of this phoneme, although it is impossible to deny the existence of this identity.

In analysing the difficulties that arise from defining the notion of structure, one notices that the epistemologist who attempts to formulate such a definition is in a situation similar to that of the phonetician. On the one hand, he cannot escape the impression that the concept of structure has an identity, but on the other he cannot avoid noting the variety of its manifestations. The term has different meanings in economics and sociology. The concept of 'social structure' is clearly not the same when used by Parsons and by Lévi-Strauss. Within the work of Lévi-Strauss himself, it is far from sure whether the term structure has the same meaning in *Les Structures Elémentaires de la Parenté* and in *Le Cru et le Cuit*. The concept of 'structural analysis' differs, to say the least, from one to the other, according to the logical character of the conceptual tools with which it is associated.

In these two cases, a strong conviction of identity is thus contradicted by the undeniable differences in its manifestations, be it in the pronunciation of the entity (r) or in the concept of structure. In summary, it could be said, to paraphrase a suggestion made by R. Pagès [45], that the concept of structure is a collection of homonyms.

It is well known (and the point will be made in more detail later) that the solution proposed by structural phonology to the problems of classical phonetics consisted in showing that an entity like (r), should be considered not from *inside*, but from *outside*; not according to its *intrinsic* properties, but according to its *relations* with its context. More accurately, while phonetics attempted to identify or define phonemes by reference to their pronunciations, the basic postulate of phonology is that they must be identified by reference to the context in which they appear. In other words, the identification of a phoneme is impossible without taking into account its *relationships* with other entities found in a language: (a), (b), (p), etc.

We shall come back to the nature of these relationships later on. At this point the important thing is to realize that whenever entities such as (a), (b), (p), etc. are identified by reference to the relationships between them, one can easily imagine a language in which all units would differ from the entities (a), (b), (p), etc., and which would not be distinct from the language whose units are defined by these entities. For this to occur it is only necessary that the system of relationships between (a), (b), (p), etc. be the same as those which govern

B

the units (a'), (b'), (p'), etc. in the second language. One could then write the equation $(p) = (p')$, even if from the phonetic or acoustic point of view the pronunciations of (p) were very different from the pronunciations of (p'). Conversely one can well imagine that $(p)_A$ may be held as different from $(p)_B$, if a 'single' entity, viewed as such by acoustics and phonetics, appeared in two languages A and B in such a manner that the system of relationships between (p) and other units would be different in language A and in language B.

It must be acknowledged that the introduction of the isomorphic concept suggested here is rather artificial, but it merely serves to stress a new analogy between the problem of defining phonemes and that of defining the concept of structure. As has already been shown, an entity like (r) may be pronounced in several ways. On the other hand, the same pronunciation of a sound can correspond to different entities, depending on whether it belongs to language A or language B. Carrying over this idea to the present problem, one could ask if concepts which are apparently synonymous with that of structure, i.e. 'pattern'*, 'system of relationships', 'whole not reducible to the sum of its parts', 'Aufbau', 'Gefüge', 'coherent system', etc., do not have relationship with the concept of structure analogous to that of $(p)_A$ to $(p)_B$. Considered intrinsically, the entities $(p)_A$ and $(p)_B$ are not distinct, nor is structure distinct from, for example, 'systems of relationships'. Considered extrinsically, they are distinct entities. This also holds if one compares externally the concept of structure with the synonyms associated with it. In other words, it can be shown that while the concept of structure inevitably evokes certain associations (structure–pattern, structure–system of relationships, etc.) it is nevertheless distinct from these terms. The relationship between 'structure' and for example 'system of relationships' is—to quote an example used by André Martinet—the same as that between the Persian word *bad* and the word *bad* in English. The two words are pronounced in exactly the same manner and are thus not *intrinsically* distinct. However there is a considerable difference between them which is only revealed by context: one is Persian and the other is English. The same is true of the

* In English in the original text.

concept of structure: in terms of its *content*, it is in some ways indistinguishable from its *associations*. However this is no longer the case when reference is made to the *contexts* in which it occurs. Finally then, rather than analysing the content of the concept of *structure*—a content which is rather banal and crude —it is necessary to investigate the role played by this concept in the contexts in which it appears.

As has been noted, the *synonyms* and *homonyms* linked in common language usage to the concept of structure produce a contradictory impression. In the case of homonyms, the contradiction lies between the identity of the concept of structure and the variety of its usages. In the case of synonyms, the contradiction is between the impossibility of inductively defining the concept of structure without making recourse to its synonymic associations, and the accompanying sense of failure experienced when reducing it to these associations. This failure is so clear that, when attempts such as Lévy's [33] or Viet's [57] are made to employ an inductive definition of the concept of structure, the result is a complete disintegration of that which makes up the very nature of this concept. It becomes impossible to distinguish between the 'structuralist methodology' common to these authors and that which could simply be termed 'the methodology' of the human sciences. In spite of thorough research and analysis, neither author was able to discover anything more to the concept of structure than its well-known associations 'structure–totality', 'structure–system of relationships', etc. This result is not surprising since the *content* of the concept of structure does reduce to these associations.

Hence the feeling that contradiction results from the *polysemic* nature of the concept of structure (an expression coined to summarize the fact that this concept is a collection of homonyms pertaining to a collection of synonymic associations) can easily be explained away if a change of perspective takes place, analogous to that in which classical phonetics gave way to structural phonology. In other words, when attempts at inductive defining have failed to show the meaning of the concept of structure, it becomes necessary to attempt an extrinsic rather than an intrinsic definition.

Thus it becomes a question not of determining the elements common to all definitions of the word 'structure' which have been propounded—such a procedure would not take one much further than the definitions by Piaget or Flament quoted earlier —but of analysing the function of the concept of structure in the scientific vocabulary of the authors who use it. Similarly a phoneme can only be defined by the discriminatory function it performs in a given language.

While it is important to stress the analogy between the problems of structural phonology and the problem discussed here, both as a guide to analysis and with a view to clarifying the text quoted from Lévi-Strauss, we have reservations about referring to the 'structural analysis' of the concept of structure. These reservations are on two grounds. Firstly, the use of such a term would result in a vicious circle in the argument. Secondly and more importantly, the idea of applying a 'structural' definition to a scientific term is so obvious that this type of definition is used spontaneously, like Molière's Bourgeois Gentilhomme who talked in prose without knowing that he did so.

The irrelevance of inductive definitions

Let us consider for example the concept of hypothesis. To find its meaning one might—though who would?—apply the inductive method: collecting a body of specific hypotheses and attempting to determine their common elements. These would indicate that hypotheses imply an uncertainty, a statement held as provisional or open to doubt. One would also find synonymic associations for this concept 'hypothesis': 'hypothesis–proposition open to doubt', 'hypothesis–provisional statement', etc. The part played by these associations would be comparable with those of 'structure–totality', 'structure–system of relationships', etc. in the case of the concept of structure. An attempt could then be made to define the concept via these associations. The pay-off from such a method would obviously be small, without its results being absurd. It is certainly true that to state a hypothesis involves both doubt and only tentative affirmation. However, to define the concept of hypothesis in this way, *intrinsically*, would prevent one from grasping the difference between this concept and its synonymic associations.

The other method, characteristic of philosophical textbooks, consists in simultaneously providing the concept of hypothesis and the concepts of proof or of verification, that is, to consider the former *extrinsically*, by way of its relationship to other terms with which it is necessarily linked.

In the same way, a structural definition of the entity (*r*) is only possible because it necessarily appears within a context. No one in normal French language usage ever made a speech limited to (*r*). Similarly no one ever made hypotheses without the intention that they should be submitted to test.

Although in some respects it is so obvious as to verge on the ridiculous, this example does clarify the basic task of analysing the concept of structure. To make a structural analysis of the concept of hypothesis consists first and foremost in outlining the function performed by this concept in a variety of contexts.

Incidentally one may wonder why an approach which seems so obvious in the case of a concept like *hypothesis* is rarely deemed necessary for the concept of structure. The statement may be ventured that Lévi-Strauss is one of the few writers who have clearly outlined this necessity.

Without going into a historical analysis, it should however be noted that the crudity of structural definitions applied to scientific terms often emerges only after a long time has elapsed.

An examination of many scientific terms shows that the structural definition of a concept may lag by decades or even centuries behind its inductive definition. Hence the debate between Leibnitz and Descartes about momentum can only appear vain today, because the attempt was being made to grasp the nature of these forces independently from their role in a system of calculation. The same is true of the concept of *axiom*. It is not long since efforts were made to define this concept from its synonyms, *untestability*, *prior given*, etc., though the commonplace stating that a deductive argument necessarily supposed a body of unproven propositions was acknowledged in the end. Of course an *axiom*, defined in terms of its intrinsic properties, is an unproven proposition. Therefore it was thought for centuries that certain propositions must be the starting point of an argument *because* they were *untestable* or *intuitively* true. The epistemological difficulties raised by the concept of axiom did not vanish until it was understood that an axiom was not a proposition placed at the beginning of a deductive argument because it was untestable—but rather a proposition made untestable by its location at the beginning of the argument. This realization surmounted the difficulties arising from the concepts of test and falsification, as well as the contradiction due to the fact that the same proposition can be stated as an axiom in one context and a demonstrable hypothesis in another.

The form taken by this epistemological revolution was simply the substitution of *extrinsic* definition of the concept axiom for an *intrinsic* one. Intrinsic definitions had described this concept by reference to an unclear characteristic: that of *undemonstrability*. On the other hand, extrinsic definitions only underline that an axiomatic proposition comes *first*, not in the sense that it is either more evident or basic, but only that it is a pre-condition of the propositions deduced from it. Similarly it could be shown that the debates around the concept of *cause* always revolve round the opposition between intrinsic and extrinsic definitions of this concept. As in the case of 'axiom', the epistemological difficulties raised by the concept of cause vanish as one passes from the former to the latter type of definition.

It should be noted in passing that all these *intrinsic* definitions —those of axiom, cause and structure—tend to use *definientia* more obscure than the term defined. Thus the concept of undemonstrability is at least as unclear as that of axiom (when defined by its intrinsic properties). Similarly the concepts of 'system of relationship', and of 'whole not reducible to the sum of its parts' are no clearer than the concept of structure (when defined by its intrinsic properties).

Despite the manifest advantages deriving from extrinsic definitions, historical examples show that they usually meet with much resistance.

Furthermore, while the method suggested to clarify the concept of structure as used in the human sciences is in principle easy to describe, it is in practice difficult to apply. Although we are well aware that the concept of hypothesis necessarily appears in contexts also including the term verification (or, to be precise, falsification in the case of experimental sciences),[2] the concept of structure is not so straightforward.

The criteria of a non-inductive definition of the concept of structure

If the concept of structure is analysed from this standpoint, means may be provided for assessing the adequacy of such an analysis.

Only if such an analysis represents a *theory*, giving as satisfactory an account as possible of the epistemological and linguistic considerations mentioned earlier, will it be valid. Thus an appropriate analysis should at the same time explain that the concept of structure involves the conjuring up of certain associations (structure–coherence, structure–whole not reducible to the sum of its parts, structure–system of relationships, etc.), and of negative associations (structure–external characteristics, structure–aggregate, etc.), and also that in many contexts it is irreducible to these associations and negative associations. It should moreover account for the existence of a collection of homonymic associations. It should thus further understanding of the reasons for which one refers to 'structural parameters' of econometric models, to 'structural description of a sentence' in the sense used by Miller [41] or Chomsky [8], [9], to 'kinship structures' in the sense used by Lévi-Strauss [31], to 'structuring of social roles' in the sense used by Parsons [47] or Nadel [44], to the 'phonological structure' of a language in the sense of Harris [21] or Jakobson [22] for example, or again to the 'structure of political systems' as used by R. Aron [1]. The same type of analysis must explain both the recent diffusion and the rapid spread of the concept of structure in the vocabulary of the human sciences.

Two types of theory present potential solutions to these questions. The first is illustrated in a passage from Kroeber [25]:

Structure appears to be just a yielding to a word that has a perfectly good meaning but suddenly becomes fashionably attractive for a decade or so—like 'streamlining'—and during its vogue tends to be applied indiscriminately because of the pleasurable connotations of its sound. . . . So what structure adds to the meaning of our phrase seems to be nothing, except to provoke a degree of pleasant puzzlement.

While this is incontestable, it remains necessary to explain how this fashion caught on, since the term 'structure' is not applied to an inappropriate object, i.e. it is not applied unless the object has a certain resemblance to a structure (the reader is asked to bear with the present vagueness of language, which cannot be avoided at this stage of the discussion). In this vein, while it would be possible to attribute to a lack of attention the fact that a listener understood:

'Gal, amant de la reine . . .'

instead of

'galamment de l'arène . . .'*,

this explanation would be incomplete unless the similarity of sounds were taken into account. The same is true of the term 'structure'. Although it seems that there is very little in common between Nadel's notion of 'structure of social roles' and Lévi-Strauss's use of the term 'kinship structure', except that social roles and kinship rules are differentiated systems and not, in Kroeber's words, 'completely amorphous'. But does the 'pleasant puzzlement' connected with the term structure provide a sufficient explanation for its use?

Even admitting the existence of fashion and its manifestations—whose influence we do not wish to minimize—the fact remains that it provides only a partial explanation. The term structure could not have become so popular in the human sciences without it designating a fundamental reference in that vocabulary. The success of second-rate writers vulgarizing ill-defined structuralism does not explain the popularity of structure as a concept. Quite the reverse: it is the real importance of this concept that accounts for its saleable value.

An alternative theory, propounded here, cuts through the homonymic associations characterizing the uses of structure, to maintain that this concept has an indisputable identity, which corresponds to a transformation in scientific vocabulary and which in the main is as remote from its synonymic associations as is the concept of hypothesis from those of 'doubtful pro-

* Quoted from a poem by Victor Hugo.

position' or 'provisional statement'. In the experimental sciences, the concept of hypothesis is only separated from its synonymic associations by scientific vocabulary itself, which does not predate Galileo. Similarly, the concept of structure is only separated from its synonymic associations by the language of the scientific theory of systems*, using the word 'scientific' in the sense employed by Karl Popper.[3]

The concept of system

This chapter will conclude with a brief consideration of the concept of system. The success and degree of influence of Galilean physics compared with the sterility of Aristotelian physics have lent credence over the centuries to the universal validity of Galileo's mechanistic model. As a result, a rather simple-minded epistemology gained favour, according to which teleological explanations should be confined to metaphysics, while science should remain the field of mechanistic explanations.

The outcome of this approach meant that many problems were placed beyond the scientific pale. Thus the phenomena of equilibrium and equilibration, characterizing systems such as markets, organisms and personalities, defied analysis since teleological explanations were to be avoided—and rightly so— in a Galilean system.

This epistemology has now been abandoned. The mathematical analysis of economic equilibria shows, for example, that tendencies towards equilibrium and re-equilibration typical of an economic system can be explained by an adequate representation of the desires and behaviour of the economic agents composing this system. Thus, while this basic behaviour may appear oriented towards the attainment of a certain end-state in the system, it is unnecessary to impute that this state was actually sought. This applies also to the biological theory of homeostasis. The work of Cannon and Sherrington demonstrated the processes by which the organism attains equilibrium, without making reference to teleological principles. In linguistics, the collation of grammatical rules, the recording and interpretation of the historical evolution undergone by a given rule

*Amended to read 'scientific theory' rather than 'scientific language'.

or phenomenon are no longer sufficient when languages can now be analysed as systems of interdependent elements whose end is to assure the accurate transmission of messages. Once again the concept of goal has been reintroduced into scientific analysis, since it is the capacity of a language as a system of signs permitting the unambiguous transmission of messages which must itself be explained. In this case the goal is explained, but is not construed as explanatory.

Most revolutions or innovations in the human sciences during the last decades have essentially been discoveries of methods that permit the analysis of systems as such. This is equally true of the Freudian personality theory, linguistics and modern anthropology, as well as of econometrics, without mentioning the obvious cases of cybernetics and *systems theory*, whose very object is the concept of system. Structural linguistics and its major innovation, i.e. the attempt to formulate a theory emphasizing the contextual coherence of sound elements or of the grammatical rules observed in natural languages, have already been mentioned. The anthropological revolution brought about by Lévi-Strauss whereby the analysis of kinship rules consists in showing that they constitute a system of coherent elements rather than being, as old-fashioned ethnographers had it, rules more or less arbitrary in nature, the products of an accumulation of haphazard occurrences, also provides a pertinent example.

The hypothesis defended here is that the growing acceptance of the concept of structure is related to the whole process of scientific change, as a result of which various disciplines have succeeded in formulating testable theories explaining the interdependence between the component elements of their subjects.

In economics, the beginning of this change can be traced back to Walras and Pareto, or possibly to Cournot, whereas in linguistics it dates back to Saussure. It was always realized, in biology, that human beings were systems, i.e. wholes irreducible to the sum of their parts. Hence the introduction by Aristotle of the famous concept of *ultimate cause*. Nevertheless experimental biology at the end of the nineteenth century still persisted in applying a mechanistic model: the experiments conducted by Claude Bernard consistently sought relationships of cause and effect. As a reaction against mechanistic biology, the metaphysical theory of *vitalism* developed. While adding nothing to our knowledge of living matter, it is of interest to the historian of science only to the extent that it indicated the inability of nineteenth-century biology to deal with organisms as such, in other words as systems. Hence at the turn of the century two theories characterized biology, the scientific but mechanistic, and the teleological but metaphysical. It is only in the twentieth century that tools have been developed which permit the scientific analysis of the end-state that appears to dominate organisms. First the theory of homeostasis, already mentioned, was formulated; it was followed by the development of new mathematical tools, like cybernetics, which permit phenomena of regulation and equilibration characteristic of living systems. From this point on, the biologist was able to analyse an organism as such (that is as a system) with the help of testable theories.

In other disciplines like sociology, concern with a theory of systems is long-standing, since its roots can be traced to Montesquieu (would we not today employ the word *structure* where Montesquieu referred to the *spirit* of laws?)[4]. However, if one considers certain branches of sociology in isolation, particularly those of micro-sociology and more generally of social psychology, it is far from certain that this discipline has succeeded in producing testable theories about social systems. Thus it appears that although the concept of structure stands for a scientific *approach* common to all the human sciences, its overtones vary according to context.

This view will be expanded in the following chapter, through the detailed analysis of some typical examples rather than an overall review—which of necessity would be superficial and incomplete—of the uses of this concept in the human sciences.

2

Two Types of Context of the Concept of Structure; Intentional Definitions

THE ambiguity surrounding the concept of structure is to a large extent explained by the fact that the word 'structure' appears in two types of profoundly different contexts.

In the first type of context, the word structure is used either to underline the systematic nature of an object—to indicate, in other words, that one is dealing with a group of interdependent variables—or to stress that a certain method is applied in order to describe an object as a system. In this case, the concept is not, strictly speaking, rooted in systems theory. For the sake of clarity, this will be described as its use in the context of an *intentional definition*. Although this type of use is very similar to the popular usage of the word structure, it is nevertheless worthy of notice. On the one hand, any analysis of the concept of structure should take into account all the functions performed by this concept. On the other, much of the confusion surrounding the concept of structure is due to the neglect of this contextual distinction.

The second type of context is characterized by the incorporation of the concept of structure within a theory attempting to account for the systematic nature of an object. In this case the word structure is used in the context of an *operative definition*.

There is an alternative and possibly simpler way of describing this distinction. In the case of an intentional definition, what is sought is the meaning of the concept of structure. In the case of an operative definition, what is involved is an attempt to determine the structure of a given object. Thus in the latter case, interest is not centred on the concept of structure itself, although the very fact of analysing the structure of an object implies that a certain meaning is given to the concept of structure. To clarify this distinction, the definition given by Piaget is quoted again: 'A structure (in the most general sense) exists when elements are united in a whole which presents certain properties as a whole and the properties of the elements are wholly or partially dependent on those of the whole.' The only aim of such a definition is to inform us of Piaget's meaning when he and his many disciples use the term structure. In other words, it is the concept of structure itself that constitutes the starting point of the discussion. One could go further and argue that while such a definition may illuminate the content of the concept of structure, it is of no help in determining the particular structure of a given object. By contrast, when Lévi-Strauss describes the 'elementary structures of kinship', the definition of the concept of structure only emerges indirectly from the analysis of a particular subject-matter. In this work it is not the concept of structure itself which constitutes the core of the study, but rather the factors relevant to kinship systems. As noted earlier, such a use of the word structure involves an implicit definition of the term structure, but one which vindicates this use. Yet the purpose is not to pinpoint the meaning of the concept of structure in itself.

The present chapter will concentrate upon analysing the functions of the concept of structure in the context of intentional definitions.

Two types of context and the distinction between them

While it is certainly true that the distinction already discussed could have been presented in more general terms, nevertheless it appears preferable to clarify the distinction between the two types of contexts by way of specific examples rather than to attempt a rigorous definition.

Let us begin with a simple case, taken from the field of sociology: the opposition between *structured groups* and *non-structured groups*, as discussed by Gurvitch [19]. Leaving aside his more detailed considerations, the following passage conveniently summarizes the distinction: 'In a *non-structured* group, possessing neither multiple hierarchies nor a precarious equilibrium between them, neither clear awareness of them nor defensive weapons for their maintenance, relationships with other groups and with society as a whole will remain fluid' (p. 36; our italicization). In contrast, structured groups, or in the words of Gurvitch, 'partial structures' are characterized by 'multiple hierarchies', a 'precarious equilibrium between them,' etc.

The function of the word 'structure' in such a context serves only to contrast two kinds of groups: on the one hand, groups or groupings characterized by a certain stability of relationships between component members, by a differentiation between, and a hierarchical organization of sub-groups and individuals; on the other, groups characterized by a contrasting fluidity of inter-member and inter-subgroup relationships (to pass over Gurvitch's discussion concerning group awareness). In such a case, the term structure has no other function than to remind us that certain groupings constitute systems of individuals whose relationships are stable, or relatively more stable than in 'non-structured' groups. The mental process which led Gurvitch to employ the term 'structure' in order to designate this distinction is more or less the following: firstly, it is noted that relationships between 'collections' of individuals can be of different types. For example, at one extreme are found 'collections' of individuals made up of persons of the same age-group or the consumers of a given product. Sometimes such 'groups' behave like 'real groups'; fairly stable hierarchies and collective goals may be detected within them, and so on. Consumers may unite to manifest their discontent, and feel united in their capacity as consumers; teenagers may adopt specific group behaviour-patterns. However in general such 'collections' represent mere abstract categories. At the other extreme, for example, the group of individuals brought together in the same firm will obviously be characterized by 'multiple hierarchies' and relatively stable relationships between these individuals. Between these two extremes fall an indefinite number of conceivable intermediary cases.

These distinctions are undoubtedly both real and useful, but their importance from our point of view is that once they have been made there is no need to employ the term 'structure' in order to designate them. It is only used in such a case for reasons of convenience, because in its most common meaning, 'structure' normally implies the associations of 'structure–system of relationships', 'structure–totality', etc. The groups described by Gurvitch as 'structured' also imply these associations: when a group has a fixed system of authority relationships and its leader is removed, the *whole* system of relationships is likely to be affected as a consequence. Such a group thus conjures up the picture of a system of mutually interdependent elements. In other words, if the term 'structure' is used in this type of context, it is because the object which is described invokes the same associations as the term structure itself. It could be concluded that in this case the significance of the concept of structure is reduced to that of its *synonymic associations*.

If this is so, there is no necessity, but only convenience, involved in employing the term structure. Indeed the same object could be designated by other terms and by speaking in this case of organization or differentiation rather than of structure. Anyway there is no point in asking whether a structured group *is* really a group possessing multiple hierarchies and an equilibrium between them, etc., since it is only by convention that one associates with the term 'structure' a group defined by such characteristics. More bluntly, it is absurd to seek the right definition for a concept like 'social structure', since I may choose to call structure that which others call organization. Provided that there is agreement on the distinctions introduced by these terms, there is no disadvantage in using one rather than the other. Similarly the term 'structure' is not necessarily attached to one particular connotation rather than another.

The same comments hold for the use of the term 'structure' in other disciplines, for instance by Goldstein in the expression *structure of the organism* (translation of *Aufbau des Organismus*) [17] or by Merleau-Ponty [39] in such expressions as 'structure of behaviour', 'structure of a situation', etc. When both authors blame associationism or mechanistic explanations of organic phenomena for not considering organisms, behaviours or situations as structures, they mean nothing more by this than the need to consider such entities as wholes irreducible to the sum of their parts, as systems of interdependent elements or as systems of relationships. Here again the meaning of the term 'structure' reduces to that of its synonymic associations. One could read and reread *Aufbau des Organismus* or *La structure du comportement* without finding any more precise definition of the term 'structure'. Hence Merleau-Ponty [39] justifies the concept of situation-structure by reference to an experiment conducted by Ruger in which 'a subject practised in carrying out successively and in systematic order the various discrete operations necessary to solve a metallic puzzle was no more capable of solving the entire puzzle than if he had had no preliminary practice'. Consequently, the use of the concept of structure ties up with the observation that 'expertise acquired in relation to one part of a situation does not apply if the same part is inserted into an unfamiliar whole' (p. 113).

Goldstein [17] demonstrates the idea of organism-structure by reference to observations such as the following: an examination of patients suffering from a lesion of one of the cortical terminals of the optic tracts shows that a partial lesion does not involve a general reorganization of the visual field; in particular, the area of maximum acuity still corresponds, as in the case of normal vision, to images projected on the *macula*. However when one of these terminals is completely destroyed and thus renders half of each retina blind, general reorganization takes place: 'The point of the outside world which appears most distinct to the patient is not that whose image is formed on the edge of the intact retina, therefore in the location of the former *macula*, but a point whose image is formed towards the interior of the intact retina' (p. 44).

The interest afforded by such observations is obvious, but it is due to their content rather than to any proof they offer that organisms, situations or behaviour patterns are structures. They only prove that these elements and entities are, as has long been known, interdependent, that the organism is a whole and that this whole is more than the sum of its parts. Thus the use of the term 'structure' in these cases is, like the preceding example, simply a witness to a synonymic association. Whoever says 'structure' means 'whole irreducible to the sum of its parts'.

While the works of Merleau-Ponty and the French translation of *Aufbau des Organismus* were in their time held to be
revelations, in neither can there be found a theory of the organism or of behaviour as systems. They merely provide a collection of observations, fascinating in themselves, which do show
that the organism reacts as a whole and that behaviour can
only be understood as a whole. But who would doubt that such
commonplaces are true?

It is a great mistake, in our view, when seeking to disentangle
the meaning of the concept of structure in the human sciences,
to consider in the same breath the works of Merleau-Ponty
and Goldstein, on the one hand, and those of Lévi-Strauss or
Chomsky, on the other. In the first case, the concept of structure appears in the context of an intentional definition. It
serves only to indicate that an object has been identified as a
system. In the second case, an operative definition is involved:
the object-system is analysed by means of a theory comparable
to those of the natural sciences. The structure of the object is
nothing else than the description resulting from the application
of such a theory. The concept of structure thus plays a fundamentally different role in the two types of contexts. These are so
different in nature that they defy any attempt at reducing them
to a common definition. Conversely, the reigning confusion
about the concept of structure can generally be attributed to
those who neglect this distinction.

While the analysis of the concept of structure in the context of
what has been called 'operative' definitions will be covered
in the last two chapters, an example of this type of context
will be given now in order to emphasize the divergence between
the two types. Imagine that a series of psychometric tests had
been administered to a population and that the following
correlation matrix had been found to obtain between the scores
on the five tests (see p. 22).

If this matrix is inspected, it appears that for example the
relationship between success on tests 2 and 3 is high while that
between tests 1 and 5 is low. Though this matrix is considered
as a group of empirical results which it suffices to record as
such, there is no difficulty in imagining that the correlation
coefficient between tests 1 and 2 could have been not 0·24,

c

Fictitious correlation matrix between five psychometric tests

Tests	1	2	3	4	5
1		0·24	0·32	0·24	0·08
2	0·24		0·48	0·36	0·12
3	0·32	0·48		0·48	0·16
4	0·24	0·36	0·48		0·12
5	0·08	0·12	0·16	0·12	

but, say, 0·37. However, upon further examination the matrix shows itself to be not an aggregate of independent results, but a system of interdependent elements. Indeed the relationships between these elements obey a strict law, as we shall see.

More accurately, such a matrix has a Spearman-type structure [54]. Without being very familiar with the technique of factor analysis[1], it is easy to state that this matrix presents a certain number of regularities. Thus if one compares the coefficients belonging respectively to the first and the second column in each line where comparison is possible, that is in lines 3, 4 and 5, one notices that the first has a constant relationship with the second: $r_{13}/r_{23} = r_{14}/r_{24} = r_{15}/r_{25} = 2/3$. This property can be ascertained to be general. It applies to all the couples of columns that one can consider: columns 1 and 2, 1 and 3, 1 and 4, 1 and 5, 2 and 3, 2 and 4, 2 and 5, 3 and 4, 3 and 5, 4 and 5.

If, having discovered this arithmetic property of the correlation matrix, one claims that it has a well-defined structure, or uses any analogous expression, the term 'structure' is employed in the context of an intentional definition. All one states in effect by using this term is that the arithmetic table presents regularities and that one element could not be modified without changing the whole, since this would destroy the general property previously observed. Yet all the elements could be modified without changing the structure. It is only necessary to choose one's modifications so that the general property outlined above is conserved. When describing this matrix as a *structure*, when saying that it has a structure, one uses expressions which have exactly the same meaning as the concepts of *form* or *Gestalt* in psychology.

Unless more is said, the term structure has a meaning no different from that used in the contexts analysed above: the matrix 'is a structure' and 'has a structure' to the extent that its elements are linked to each other by well-determined relationships and are dependent upon a general property characterizing the group of elements as a whole. The use of the term 'structure' again only refers us back to the familiar synonymic associations: 'structure–whole' or 'structure–dependence of elements in relation to the whole'.

However, the situation changes when one asks why a correlation matrix derived from a series of psychometric tests can have such a structure (although it is exceptional in practice to find matrices conforming to the property described above as strictly as this one does, cases where this condition is approximately met are less rare). At this stage, a theory of the object-system represented by the matrix must be attempted.

The theory Spearman applied to this type of result is too well known to require spelling out. Let us assume that the results obtained by a given subject on a specific test were dependent on a factor or an aptitude systematically called upon by the tests administered. In other words, the hypothesis is advanced that the level of success of each subject on each test depends upon a general ability which each of these subjects possesses in different degrees. This hypothesis only presents in an abstract way an operation frequently performed in daily life: when we say that Peter *is* dull-witted, astute, subtle, we wish to indicate that each time he is confronted by a certain type of test, he will tend to react in a certain way, that is to be in general more dull-witted, or more astute, or more subtle than Paul. Similarly, when a series of psychometric tests are administered to a group of subjects, certain of them will succeed better than others. Put another way, the degree of success at one test permits the prediction of results on a second test, with a margin of error depending upon the similarity between the two tests. Returning to the correlation matrix presented on p. 22, it appears that tests 2 and 3 are somewhat alike, since the correlation coefficient between performance on both is high. On the other hand, the coefficient between the scores gained on tests 2 and 5 being low indicates that these tests have less in common with one another than have tests 3 and 4. Spearman hypothesizes that when one notes the existence of a 'structure' of intercorrelations analogous to that of our example, this means that the tests all tap a certain basic ability, but do so to different degrees.

To clarify this point, let us posit, as Spearman himself does, that this general ability is *intelligence* and that success at tests administered depends upon it. By designating the score of an individual as z_{ij} for individual i on test j, and by G_i the score—unknown—of individual i in terms of this general ability, the hypothesis consists in stating that z_{ij} is a function of G_i. On the other hand, it is clear that success at a test cannot be conceived of as depending on a single ability systematically tapped. Certain tasks will have additional effects upon given subjects because of their particular content. To express this hypothesis, it is stated that z_{ij} is a function not only of G_i, but also of specific factors e_{ij} whose effect varies, as the multiple index indicates, with the specific test and given subjects used.

Hence it is necessary to relate z_{ij} to both G_i and e_{ij}; and as it is reasonable to choose the simplest possible function linking them, it is posited that the relationship is linear. One would thus write:

$$z_{ij} = a_j G_i + e_{ij}.$$

Coefficient a_j represents the importance of general ability G in task j and therefore will vary from test to test. If G stands for intelligence and for example test a_2 measures this to a greater extent than does a_3, this means that intelligence will play a greater part in bringing about success on test 2 than on test 3, success on the latter being due to a greater extent to secondary factors e.

Certain conventions are standardized for the measurement of z and G. Since it is reasonable to suppose that a score on a test or on an aptitude test is a matter of convention, the numerical range to which scores are fitted can be arbitrarily selected. It is convenient to standardize scores around the mean. Suppose for example that the mean is 13 on test j, the score of a subject who achieved 15 will be recorded as 2, i.e. this representing his deviation from the mean. Obviously the mean of all deviation scores will be equal to zero. Accordingly if the scores z_{1j}, $z_{2j} \ldots z_{nj}$ are added for subjects no. 1, 2, . . . n on test j, as deviations from the mean:

$$z_{1j} + z_{2j} + \ldots + z_{nj} = 0.$$

this expression can also be written more neatly by using the symbol for summation Σ, in the form:

$$\sum_i z_{ij} = 0.$$

Naturally G_i, which is the hypothetical measure of intelligence postulated by the theory, cannot be observed directly. However nothing prevents one from assuming that this factor can also be measured in terms of deviation from its mean. Consequently if G_1 is the *intelligence* of subject no. 1, G_2 the intelligence of subject no. 2, and so on until subject n, we can postulate that:

$$G_1 + G_2 + \ldots + G_n = 0.$$

Again this can be summarized more neatly as:

$$\sum G_1 = 0.$$

In the same way that an arbitrary origin has been chosen for measurement, units of measurement may also be arbitrarily selected. Without going into details, it is convenient to choose as a unit of measurement the mean of the squares of the scores registered by n individuals. Thus if one considers test j for example, one can write the following:

$$\frac{1}{n} 2^2{}_{1j} + 2^2{}_{2j} + \ldots + 2^2{}_{nj} = 1.$$

Similarly such a formula can be written out for measures of intelligence

$$\frac{1}{n} (G_1 + G^2{}_2 + \ldots G^2{}_n) = 1.$$

The last two expressions may be summarized as follows:

$$\frac{1}{n} \sum 2^2{}_{ij} = \frac{1}{n} \sum G^2{}_i = 1.$$

On the other hand, it follows from the theory described earlier that the influence of the secondary factors e_j are independent from the general factor G, and that the effects of the secondary factors are independent from one test to the other. Consequently there should be no correlations between G and each of the secondary factors e_j. Also there should be no correlation between each of the secondary factors e_j and any other of them.

Let us consider, for example, the specific factors involved in the execution of tests j and k and let us assume that one can measure these factors. To clarify the example, suppose that test j involves a spatial ability and that e_{ij} is the aptitude of subject i in this respect. In test k it is a completely different specific ability which is required. The hypothesis is that there will be no correlation between the scores (unknown) e_{1j}, $e_{2j} \ldots e_{nj}$, on the one hand, and the scores (unknown) e_{1k}, $e_{2k} \ldots e_{nk}$ on the other. According to our conventions, this hypothesis is expressed by the following equation[2]:

$$\frac{1}{n}(e_{1j}e_{1k} + e_{2j}e_{2k} + \ldots + e_{nj}e_{nk}) = 0.$$

This equation is obviously correct whatever the two tests j and k may be. In the same way, since intelligence G is assumed to be independent from the secondary abilities e_j involved in a given test, one can write:

$$\frac{1}{n}(e_{1j}G_1 + e_{2j}G_2 + \ldots + e_{nj}G_n) = 0.$$

The preceding equations can be contracted as follows:

$$\frac{1}{n}\sum e_{ij}e_{ik} = \frac{1}{n}\sum e_{ij}G_i = 0 \text{ (for any } j).$$

All these hypotheses merely specify further the theory whereby success at different tests depends upon a general ability. If they are admitted, the correlation r_{jk} between the scores on the two tests j and k is expressed (in contracted form) by the following:

$$r_{jk} = \frac{1}{n}\sum_i 2_{ij}2_{ik} = \frac{1}{n}\sum_i (a_jG_i + e_{ij})(a_kG_i + e_{ik}) =$$
$$\frac{1}{n}(a_ja_k\sum_i G_i + a_j\sum G_ie_{ik} + a_k\sum G_ie_{ij} + \sum_i e_{ij}e_{ik}).$$

However, because of the above hypotheses,

$$\frac{1}{n} \sum_i G_i = 1$$

and

$$\frac{1}{n} \sum_i G_i e_{ik} = \frac{1}{n} \sum_i G_i e_{ij} = \frac{1}{n} \sum_i e_{ij} e_{ik} = 0.$$

Hence the only consequence of interest to us in explaining the arithmetic properties of the matrix given in the example is

$$r_{jk} = a_j a_k.$$

Let us call two elements appearing in the same line of the matrix r_{31} (third line, first column) and r_{32} (third line, second column). With reference to the preceding equation, $r_{31} = a_3 a_1$ and $r_{32} = a_3 a_2$. Consequently the relationship between the two elements is that of a_1/a_2. The same goes for the correlations appearing in other lines (belonging respectively to the same columns). Thus $r_{41} = a_4 a_1$ and $r_{42} = a_4 a_2$. The same holds for the coefficients r_{51} and r_{52}. The same property can be found for all couples of columns.

When one states that the correlation matrix provided in the example has a Spearman structure, one implies that the arithmetic properties of this matrix can be explained by a theory, or more precisely that they can be expressed as logical consequences of a set of theoretical propositions or axioms.

This example has therefore a different logical status from those which were quoted earlier. In this case the term 'structure' does not indicate that the object considered *is* a system and should be treated as such. Instead it denotes success in applying a logical construct to account for the observable characteristics of the system. While in the examples quoted from Gurvitch, Goldstein or Merleau-Ponty the term 'structure' was applied to an object, here it characterizes a logical model. Thus the statement that the matrix considered is unifactorial in structure signifies that the properties of this matrix may be due to the operation of the main principle of the theory, hypothesizing the existence of a unique and general factor or ability.

To make matters clearer, in the example provided by

Gurvitch the meaning of the concept of structure reduces to a statement of its synonymic associations. In the case cited from Spearman the meaning of the term cannot ultimately be understood without reference to the logical construct or theory from which it cannot be dissociated.

The fact that Gurvitch and Merleau-Ponty use the same term, 'structure', in relation to very different phenomena is understandable since both authors only seek either to underline the systematic nature of an object or to denote that the synonymic associations of the term 'structure' are relevant in a given context. However, the fact that Spearman and Lévi-Strauss use the same term in relation to different phenomena can only be explained by comparing the logical constructs associated with the theory of intelligence-testing and the analysis of kinship structures: if the same term is used, then the constructs must have basic characteristics in common. What they do have in common is easy to detect—the concept of structure appears in the context of a hypothetico-deductively testable theory applied to a system. The purpose of such a theory is to account for the interdependence of the elements of the given system or, in other words, the set of relationships which characterize it.

Incidentally it would be unwise to conclude prematurely from the single example of an operative definition given above that the concept of structure necessarily implies a mathematical *model* in this type of context. For this reason care has been taken in the foregoing to avoid the term *model* and employ the less precise expression *logical construct*. While it is true that one cannot refer to a 'Spearman structure' without recourse to a mathematical model, as will be shown in the following chapter, the term structure often does appear in the context of an operative definition without the hypothetico-deductive theory involved being a 'model' in the strict sense.

While still on the subject of operative definitions of the concept of structure (to be discussed more fully in the next chapter), one possible objection may be briefly tackled. Some may object that the difference between the examples of intentional definitions given and that of Spearman lies in the vagueness of the former. The answer is that while the definitions given to the concept of structure by Gurvitch are certainly not very clear (by which unambiguous criteria could it be decided whether a group was structured or not?), examples of intentional definitions linked with rigorous criteria, even some of a mathematical kind, can be produced. Conversely, as will be shown in the last chapter, many instances can be given of definitions which must be categorized as operative—because they are related to deductive theories applied to object-systems—and which nevertheless remain unrigorous.

Further examples of the concept of structure in the context of an intentional definition

To demonstrate that the concept of structure can appear in the context of an intentional definition and be unambiguously defined, two examples will be analysed. The first is borrowed from Blau [4], the second from Lazarsfeld and Menzel [29].

Both examples originate in methodological research undertaken in connection with the sociological application of survey techniques. Initially, during the phase of 'atomistic' surveys, investigators were content to collect from each individual interviewed a certain amount of personal data and to subsequently analyse the inter-relationships between this data. Thus in public-opinion polling the current practice is to analyse the relationship between such variables as age, sex, income, socio-economic category and political preferences. As Blumer [5] has shown, such polling produces purely abstract results in so far as individuals are considered independently from their social environment. Hence the growing trend among contemporary sociologists towards 'contextual' surveys, integrating not only individual variables, but also variables characterizing the individual's environment. This type of survey takes up a hint which can be found in Durkheim's *Suicide*. In the pages devoted to an analysis of the relationship between suicide and divorce, Durkheim remarked that the sex differentials in suicide rates are a function of the availability of divorce in the community. In Berlin, Brandenburg, East Prussia, and Saxony, where divorce was very frequent at the time, the number of suicides committed by married men was in a ratio of 1·80 to 1 suicide committed by a married woman. This ratio fell to a little over 1:2 in the German provinces where divorce was less frequent, and to under 1:1 in those where it was rare. This held not only for Germany, but for all the other countries from which Durkheim was able to collect statistical data. In this analysis the relationship between two individual variables (sex and suicide) and a collective or contextual variable (relationship between the number of divorces and the number of married individuals) is involved. Whenever such contextual variables can be constructed, a considerable refinement is added to sociological analysis, since individuals are no longer considered in isolation from the social environment. It is in this connection that Blau introduces the concept of 'structural effect'.

To clarify the concept of 'structural effect' as defined by Blau [4], let us imagine a survey involving only four variables. For the first variable two values, X and $\bar{X}$, are recorded among the individuals in a given population. Each individual in the population may, in other words, be attributed either label X or label $\bar{X}$. For the second variable two values Y and $\bar{Y}$ are recorded among the same individuals. In addition two variables are recorded for the sub-groups within the wider general population: the first is the proportion x of individuals who possess the characteristic X in each sub-group. The second, designated by y, represents the proportion of individuals who possess characteristic Y in each sub-group.

Although these definitions are purely formal and refer to situations commonly encountered in the analysis of sociological surveys, it will further clarify matters to lend a concrete interpretation to these variables. This will be done by reference to the famous example of the relationship between suicide and religion, analysed in Durkheim's *Suicide*. Variable X divides the population into those possessing the characteristic X (Protestant affiliation) and those possessing characteristic $\bar{X}$ (non-Protestant affiliation). Variable x is thus defined as the proportion of Protestants in a given geographical area, be it (as in Durkheim) Prussian provinces, Swiss cantons and French *départements*, or any other conglomeration of geographical units. Variable y represents the proportion of individuals who have committed suicide within a given geographical area.

Variables X and x are explanatory or *independent*. Variable y

is to be explained or treated as *dependent*. Variable Y is a simple *auxiliary* that only serves to construct y. In other words, it remains to discover if the proportion of suicides varies with religious affiliation and with the proportion of individuals of a given affiliation within a given area.

These variables having been defined, one may observe several types of influence of the independent variables on the dependent variables. Some of these were called structural effects by Blau. In order to clarify the meaning of the concept of structure in this case, the typology within the framework in which it is used must be briefly outlined first.[3]

The following effects may theoretically be observed in the research design described (bearing in mind that these effects can be detected in a wide variety of cases and that their specific application to suicide is only intended for clarification).

1. *The individual effect*

The individual effect is evident when analysis shows that, for example, Protestants commit suicide more frequently than non-Protestants, when the rate of suicide in the two groups is independent from their proportional representation in the environment studied. If this situation is represented graphically in the space delineated by the axes x (proportion of Protestants) and y (proportion of suicides), the curves characterizing Protestants and non-Protestants respectively will run parallel to one another and to the x axis. This is shown diagrammatically in figure 1a.

2. *The collective effect*

This corresponds to the case, rather paradoxical in the context of the present example, but common enough in other situations, in which the rate of suicide would depend upon the characteristics of the environment (proportion of Protestants) without Protestants and non-Protestants having different suicide rates in the same environment. Supposing that the function $y = f(x)$ linking the proportion of Protestants and the suicide rate is linear, this situation is represented by two lines superimposed upon each other and not parallel to the x axis (figure 1b).

3. *Juxtaposition of the individual effect and the collective effect*

In such cases the suicide rate would be thought to vary with *x* (proportion of Protestants in the community) for the two groups of individuals. Furthermore the suicide rate is dependent on *X*. Thus in all cases Protestants commit suicide more frequently than non-Protestants. However the collective effect does not influence the individual effect. The result is as if the two effects were cumulative in every possible situation. On the other hand, the individual variable does not influence the collective effect. This situation may be represented by two distinct lines which are parallel to each other, but not to the *x* axis (figure 1*c*). If the individual effect is measured by the distance between the two lines, it appears that its value is constant, regardless of the value of *x*. In other words, the fact of being Protestant involves a greater propensity to suicide, whatever the proportion of Protestants in the community. Similarly, the collective effect is measured by the angle of the two lines—since they are parallel, the angles are equal. Consequently the collective effect is independent from the individual variable *X* and the increase in the suicide rate as a function of the increase in number of Protestants is the same, whether one considers Protestants or non-Protestants.

4. *The individual effect and the collective effect compounded*

In this case the suicide rate varies with *x* for both groups of individuals. It also varies with *X*. Stated verbally, the suicide rate varies with the proportion of Protestants in the community and with religious affiliation. But a new fact intervenes: the variation of *y* in relation to *x* is itself dependent on *X*. Where this is linear, the situation can be represented by two non-parallel lines (figure 1*d*).

Blau gives the name of 'structural effects' to the effects pertaining to types 2, 3 and 4. What interests us in this connection is why the concept of structure has been introduced in relation to these types of effects.

Formally a *structural* effect is thus one which betrays the influence on individual behaviour of a property which, although

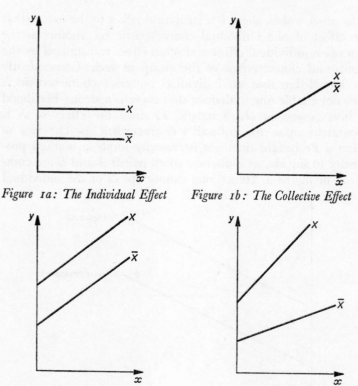

Figure 1a: The Individual Effect   *Figure 1b: The Collective Effect*

Figure 1c: The juxtaposition of   *Figure 1d: The Individual Effect*
the Individual and the   *and the Collective Effect*
Collective Effects   *compounded*

Figure 1: Typology of the effects of a dichotomous individual variable
and a continuous collective variable on an individual variable (from
Davis [11], [12])

it does not pertain to any individual in particular, characterizes the given group of individuals as such:

The general principle is that if ego's X affects not only ego's Y but also alter's Y, a structural effect will be observed which means that the distribution of X in a group is related to Y even though the individual's X is constant. Such a finding indicates that the network of relations in the group with respect to X influences Y. It isolates the effects on X on Y that are entirely due to or transmitted by the processes of social interaction. (Blau [4], p. 64)

In other words, there is a structural effect to the extent that
the effect of one individual characteristic on another is the
sum of an individual effect and of an effect transmitted by the
group and characteristic of the group as such. Consequently
the knowledge that an individual possesses characteristic X
does not enable one to deduce that there is a strong likelihood
of him possessing characteristic Y, since the effect of X is
dependent upon the collective characteristic x. The fact of
being a Protestant does not necessarily imply a marked propensity to suicide, as is obvious when points A and B are compared in figure 2. Hence one cannot speak of the individual

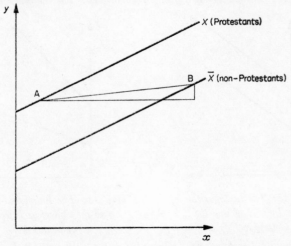

*Figure 2: One can only refer to the 'Individual' effect of X on Y,
if individuals sharing the same value of x are compared*

effect of X on Y unless the *collective* part of the effect of X on Y
is controlled by a comparison, e.g., between two groups sharing
a common value for x.

The interdependence between the individual characteristic X
and the collective characteristic x is still clearer in the case of
figure 1*d*, in relation to which the situations represented in
figures 1*b* and 1*c* appear as special cases.

In this case, the 'structural effect' is nothing other than the
effect of 'interaction', in the statistical sense of the term. In

other words the effect of the individual explanatory variable X on the individual variable Y itself depends upon the collective variable x. Symmetrically the effect of the collective variable x on the individual explanatory variable Y which one seeks to explain depends itself on the individual explanatory variable X. To clarify this idea, let us imagine an extreme case of interaction where the lines characterizing two sub-populations in terms of an individual variable intersect (figure 3). In this case

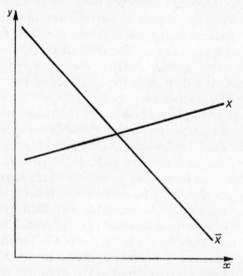

Figure 3: An example of interaction: the sign of the effect of each of the two explanatory variables depends upon the value of the other variable

it is obvious that the effect of the individual variable cannot be dissociated from the effect of the collective variable: Protestants do not commit suicide more frequently unless their concentration in the population is low.

An alternative method, though a less precise one, of defining this type of structural effect would consist in saying that in such a case the effects of the explanatory individual variable and of the explanatory collective variable are compounded rather than juxtaposed. It should be remembered at this stage that the distinction between compounding and juxtaposing is under-pinned by a formal unambiguously defined distinction.

Ultimately the thought process leading to the concept of 'structural effect' can be reconstituted as follows. Blau's starting point and that of the methodological research quoted can be traced to the concepts and procedures used in Durkheim's *Suicide*: On the one hand, under the title of 'collective conscience' Durkheim introduced the difficult notion of a transcendental social determinism. On the other hand, he produced statistical tables which cannot be ignored and which point to the operation of collective effects independent from individual determinism. Rather than speculating on the difficult concept of 'collective conscience' one should analyse the underlying statistical relationships. We then note the existence of two particularly interesting effects which correspond to the juxtapositioning and more generally to the *compounding* of individual and collective effects. In the example used it is impossible to explain the effect of an individual explanatory variable without isolating the collective effects that give rise to it. If the two effects are *compounded*, it is even impossible to explain them separately since the individual effect is a function of the collective effect, and vice versa. It is thus understandable why Blau speaks of *structural effects*: because the individual effect of X on Y has no meaning unless mediated by the influence of the distribution of X, which characterizes the group as such. In other words, this type of effect can be considered as the statistical symbol of the interdependence between the individual elements and the whole which they comprise. Thus it is because these effects evoke the associations 'structure–system of relationships', 'structure–dependence of elements on the whole', etc., that they are called 'structural'.

Let us be quite explicit. Undoubtedly when one compares terms like 'structural effect' (Blau) and, for example, 'structured group' (Gurvitch), the former definition is much more precise than the latter; in other words it is possible to determine unambiguously whether an effect is 'structural' in the sense of Blau, while one may hesitate in deciding if a group is 'structured' in the sense of Gurvitch. Nevertheless one may ask why Blau wishes to apply the term 'structural' to the effect illustrated by figures 1*b*, 1*c* and 1*d*, and not to the effect illustrated by figure 1*a*. It must be admitted that he is using an implicit definition of the term structure. Furthermore, if this definition were made explicit it would only be translated into the familiar synonymic associations 'structure–system of relations', 'structure–dependence of the parts on the whole', etc.

The meaning of the concept of structure in this context is thus formally identical with that found in the examples quoted earlier from Gurvitch, Goldstein or Merleau-Ponty. The underlying context is that of an intentional definition. The *meaning* of the concept of structure merely attests to its synonymic associations. Its role is simply to designate an object as a system.

One may state by way of proof that there would be no difficulty in replacing the word 'structure' by another term. In this connection it should be noted that the type of effect termed 'structural' by Blau has been identified under a variety of titles in sociological literature. Hence Davis [11], [12] speaks of compositional effects to designate the 'structural effects' of Blau. Lazarsfeld [26], [27] prefers to speak of 'contextual effects' to designate the group of effects represented in figures 1*b*, 1*c* and 1*d*. Occasionally the term 'structural effect' is used by that author to designate the specific type of effect illustrated by figure 1*d*.

If one asks why the sociologist considers it appropriate to speak of structural effects where the statistician would speak of *additive* effects (figure 1*c*) or *interaction* effects (figure 1*d*), a simple answer may be provided, namely that such effects take on a special meaning for the sociologist. When they are detected it signifies that the environment and the individual characteristics must be conceived of as forming a system of determinants of individual behaviour. Finally we should note that it is these effects that underlie in part the meaning of the expression 'social structure' as used in the mainstream of sociology.[4]

Another related example is the distinction introduced by Lazarsfeld and Menzel [29] between on the one hand 'structural' variables and on the other 'analytic' and 'global' variables. This example is drawn, like the previous one, from the methodological discussion arising from the analysis of social surveys.

D

When one examines the manner in which a 'variable' characterizing a group, a collectivity, a territorial unit, an institution, or any other grouping of individuals is composed, several categories may be distinguished. Firstly, some characteristics do not refer to the individual members of the 'collectivity'. Thus if one classes a group of countries in terms of the proportion of national budget devoted to defence or education, one would have defined a *global* characteristic. Secondly, collective characteristics can be found which are made up from the individual properties of members. Thus when Durkheim categorized the Swiss cantons in terms of the proportion of Protestants in their population or when one classifies a group of societies in terms of unequal income-distribution, these characteristics will be called *analytical*. Finally, characteristics can be distinguished to which Lazarsfeld and Menzel give the name of *structural*. These are made up not from the individual characteristics of component members, but from data on the *relations* between those members. An example would be to classify a number of groups according to the greater or lesser concentration of sociometric choices characterizing them.

Leaving aside an examination of the exhaustiveness and utility of this classification, all that concerns us here is that in this context, like in the previous one, the concept of structure is associated with a completely unambiguous definition, even though its meaning once again reduces to an attestation of a synonymic association of the word 'structure'. For if one asks why the third type of variable rather than the other two is entitled 'structural', it must be recognized that it is simply because the concept of structure evokes the notion of 'system of relationships'. These characteristics are rooted in basic data referring to relations between members of a collectivity. It is in this third case that the term 'structure' springs most readily to mind.

Hence it is clear that the term structure is no more indispensable in this context than it was in the examples provided by Blau and Gurvitch. In all these cases of intentional definitions where the meaning of the concept of structure reduces to an avowal of its synonymic associations, one can easily imagine that the use of a substitute terminology would not give rise to any difficulty in comprehension.

The role of the concept of structure in the context of intentional definitions

The preceding examples suffice to show that there is a type of context in which the term structure has no other significance than underlining that an object should be treated as a system. Most frequently the term structure appears in this type of context in *opposition* to other terms. It serves to indicate that certain categories of objects or certain ways of perceiving objects are opposed to others, the former evoking the synonymic associations of the term structure, while the latter do not. Thus Lazarsfeld and Menzel oppose *structural* characteristics to non-structural (global or analytic) ones, because the former refer to a group of individuals as a system of relationships. For example, when a group is described as characterized by many cliques, such a statement refers to a property characterizing the inter-individual relationships pertaining to the group. 'Structure' is thus precisely equivalent to 'system of relationships.' Similarly, Blau contrasts 'structural' and 'non-structural' effects to underline that in the first case individual and collective characteristics are juxtaposed or compounded in an explanatory *system* of individual behaviour: a structural effect exists where the individual effect of X on Y is mediated by the group. One can also refer back to the distinction introduced by Gurvitch between structured and non-structured groups and to the concepts of 'structure of behaviour' and 'structure of the situation' which Merleau-Ponty opposes to mechanistic or associationist interpretations. Here the *structural* perspective is contrasted with theories which define behaviour as a collection of reflexes or as the product of basic training, and a situation as the sum of stimuli. Such a perspective is structural to precisely the degree that it stresses the whole being greater than the sum of its parts, being anterior to the elements which compose it, etc.

Therefore in all cases where the term 'structure' appears in an oppositional context of this kind, its definition is of the *intentional* type. Its meaning reduces to an attestation of the synonymic associations of the concept of structure.

To take another example, let us consider the opposition between structure and conjuncture. The definition of these two terms varies considerably from author to author. It gives rise to

heated disputes that seem to assume the possibility of unambiguously deciding what is conjunctural and what is structural in an
economic or social system. However, if the opposition between
the two is schematized, it can be argued that there is a tendency
to consider as *structural* those characteristics of an economic or
social system which display a certain degree of permanence
over a given period and as conjunctural those which are variable
over the same period. In this sense the former are more basic
than the latter, since they characterize the system as such and
determine the limits of variation for the conjunctural characteristics.

It could be objected that this definition is a little cavalier and
underestimates the difficulties created by the concepts of 'structure' and 'conjuncture'. The reply would be that the problem
involved here is not to resolve the terminological difficulties of
particular disciplines, but simply to disentangle the meaning of
the concept of structure. In this perspective it would be perfectly useless to determine this meaning in the context of the
opposition 'structure–conjuncture' by analysing the definitions
offered by economists or by sociologists. A thorough analysis
would show that there are as many definitions as authors, and
hence one must conclude here as elsewhere that the concept of
structure is fundamentally *polysemous*. On the other hand, the
confusion and difficulty derived from the polysemic nature of
the term 'structure' in the context of the opposition 'structure–
conjuncture' disappears if the following two propositions are
accepted. Firstly, when observing a social or economic system it
is often useful to distinguish between the permanent and the
variable characteristics (this distinction of course being relative
to a period of time under consideration). Secondly, this distinction prompts one to use the term structure to designate the permanent characteristics of the system: by virtue of their stability,
they must be considered as basic conditions that control and
limit change, and as characteristic traits of the system itself. In
assenting to these two propositions, one will simultaneously
realize that the distinction is useful in scientific discourse, but
that it may give rise to a variety of definitions.

Indeed it would be incomprehensible if the concept of structure were anything but *polysemous* in this context. The character-

istics which are selected as structural depend upon the length of the period considered, the explanatory theory employed, and other factors. There is thus no reason to expect that a single definition of the concept of structure could be identified in such a context. *A fortiori* it is hopeless to expect that the word 'structure' would have a single meaning in all contexts. Hence the absurdity of trying to rely on linguistic analysis for a definition of the concept of structure that will be acceptable to all. The very attempt to seek a single definition in this way shows that the meaning of this term has not been understood.

Ultimately the divergence between these definitions does not prevent the intended distinction between structure and conjuncture from being perfectly clear. Though the debate on what should be considered as structural is very heated, this does not only imply lack of clarity in the meaning of the concept of structure in a given context.

Another couple of oppositional concepts which also give rise to much argument can be submitted to the same form of analysis. These are the two opposed sociological terms *structure* and *organization*, which have already been mentioned. On the one hand, one could list those who hold the same position as Kroeber [25], who identifies these two terms clearly and simply: 'The term "social structure" which is tending to replace "social organization" without appearing to add either content or emphasis of meaning . . .' (p. 105). On the other hand, numerous texts could be cited attempting to establish the difference between the two terms. Here again one would doubtless find as many definitions as authors, and an analysis of their content would not enable one to disentangle the meaning of the concept of structure in this type of context. At the same time the scientific intent underlying the opposition 'structure–organization' can easily be understood. If one looks at the work of Gurvitch merely as one author among many, it is clear that for him structure and organization are not synonymous. Groups can be 'structured' without at the same time being 'organized'. The 'organizations' through which a 'social class' expresses itself may be modified without the structure of the class being correspondingly changed. Briefly the *organization* of a class need not coincide with its structure.

These statements are undoubtedly vague, but the intention underlying the opposition is clear. The term 'structure' is used to underline the fact that a social system can have one form of outward *organization* (or one form of *structure*) and another inner one. For example, a system which is democratic at the level of its explicit rules of procedure may behave like an authoritarian system. If the sociologist goes no further than an analysis of appearances, it is impossible for him to understand occurrences within this system. The function of the opposition 'structure–organization' is to draw attention to such distinctions. However, when the reality and the importance of this distinction has been accepted, the use of the word 'structure' is redundant. Any number of other terms could be used, instead of opposing 'structure' and 'organization', to distinguish for example several levels of organization. It is therefore equally legitimate to argue with Kroeber that the word 'structure' has no utility provided that the distinctions referred to are expressed by other terms, and alternatively to employ this term as Gurvitch does.

On the other hand, even if the advantage of opposing 'structure' and 'organization' is recognized, no two authors would be found who define in the same way the meaning of these two terms when applied to particular subjects. However, one could safely predict that the elements grouped under the term 'structure' would always be those which are considered fundamental for the explanation of phenomena occurring within the social system. Again the word 'structure' is used because it recalls *inter alia* the synonymic association which can be summed up by the expression 'structure–essence' or by the opposition 'inner structure–outward appearance': a group with a democratic organization which functions in an authoritarian way is not democratic, but autocratic.

When the word 'structure' appears in the context of an intentional definition without being opposed to other terms, its function is even simpler, as has been said with reference to several examples. It only serves to recall certain synonymic associations in relation to an object, or a way in which an object can be considered. Most frequently its use merely points to the fact that an object is viewed as a system or as a whole which must be grasped in order to understand its parts.

In some cases an explicit reference is made to synonymic associations, as when Radcliffe-Brown [52] postulates the identity of the concepts of 'social structure' and 'system of social relationships'. In other cases, the implicit reference can usually be traced without difficulty. For example when the 'structural analysis of groups' is mentioned, it refers to all the techniques borrowed from matrix algebra and graph theory which are used to analyse the information contained in a sociogram[5]. Here again the word 'structure' only serves to remind us that the basic information dealt with takes the form of *relationships* and that the aim of analysis is to determine the properties characterizing the system of relationships as such.

In these two examples, as in earlier ones, the meaning of the word 'structure' can be reduced to its synonymic associations. Consequently 'structure' appears in such contexts as a useful term, but not as essential. Radcliffe-Brown explicitly states, by the very definition he employs, that the term 'structure' could by replaced by that of 'system of relationships' without causing any difficulty. Similarly one could speak of 'analysis of systems of inter-individual relationships' where, more briefly, 'structural analysis of groups' is used.

Obviously the remarks made earlier in the context of oppositional definitions about the difficulty of gaining a unanimously acceptable definition (in spite of the clarity of this concept) again hold here. Whereas Radcliffe-Brown defined the concept of social structure by identifying it with the 'system of social relationships', Mannheim [35] defined it as 'the web of interacting social forces from which have arisen the various modes of observing and thinking'.

Evans-Pritchard [13] for his part limits the concept of social structure to relationships between groups, explicitly excluding inter-individual relationships. Many more examples could be quoted without providing any evidence of a *common denominator* which could be subsequently used as a general definition of the concept of structure; they would merely show that the meaning given to this concept is a necessary function of the context in which it appears.

Ultimately, then, it is essential to understand that because such concepts as *social structure, structure* (in opposition to conjuncture) or *structure* (in opposition to organization) cannot be reduced to a single definition, this does not imply that the concept does not have a clear meaning. Paradoxical as this statement may seem, it could be argued that to grasp the meaning of the concept of structure one must first recognize its essentially polysemic character.

The meaning of the concept of structure in the context of intentional definitions

A metaphysical hypothesis is surreptitiously introduced when— from observing that there are nearly as many definitions of the terms 'social structure', 'economic structure', 'psychic structure' as there are sociologists, economists or psychologists—one draws the conclusion that the concept of structure has no meaning. This hypothesis can be formulated in the following manner: because such expressions as 'social structure', 'economic structure' and so on exist, they must correspond to objects in reality which are amenable to an unambiguous definition. Without this underlying hypothesis, the virulent arguments which abound in the attempt to determine the correct definition of a concept like 'social structure' would be incomprehensible.

Thus how could one state, as does Gurvitch [19] that one definition is better than another without supposing that something like a *social structure* exists in reality and that ultimately the object of the exercise is to describe it faithfully? Again we are faced with the naïve belief that structures exist in reality and can be more or less easily found and identified.

However, there is no need to resort to this hypothesis. It has already been shown that the concept of structure may be considered, in the context of intentional definitions, as having a single meaning whose specific applications vary with the area in which it is employed. The apparent existence of homonyms is thus nothing but a product of the context in which terms are used. Thus it follows that the use of the term 'structure', in whatever context, corresponds to a function which can easily be described. Hence in all cases this term serves to indicate that an object is considered as a system, or to oppose the systems approach to that view which characterizes an object as an aggregate. It follows that the word 'structure' in this type of context is like the phonemes of structural phonology: the sounds which begin the words 'kilo' and 'courage' are, from the acoustic and phonetic point of view, very different, as the reader can realize when pronouncing them. However, they will be considered as particular pronunciations of a single phoneme, the phoneme (k), to the extent that the distinction is closely correlated with context.

The situation is formally akin to this in the case of the concept of structure. Sometimes it appears in oppositional-type contexts. The specific meaning attached to it thus depends on the term to which 'structure' is opposed. Clearly the word 'structure' cannot be defined in the same way if it is opposed to 'conjuncture', to 'organization' or to 'aggregate' (as in the case of the opposition between 'atomistic survey' and 'structural survey'[6]). However the concept assumes a well delineated role in all such cases: that of distinguishing those elements which are most basic to a system, of underlining the systemic character of an object etc.

As a rule, when structure is used within the context of any oppositional definition, its meaning varies. Thus it is insufficient to accept the need for a theoretical distinction which can be— though it does not have to be—expressed by the opposition 'structure–organization', so as to be able to unambiguously decide what should be attributed to the *structure* and what relates to the *organization* in a given social system. Furthermore, even assuming distinctions were made sufficiently clear for one to be able to neatly assign all the elements of a social system to the two categories defined above (an unlikely occurrence in practice), it would still be necessary to make a choice between these elements. However, such a choice can only be made on the basis of certain antecedent postulates. In addition, these postulates themselves may be more or less prone to warrant unanimous acceptance.

Finally, the synonymic associations evoked by the word 'structure' can vary from one context to the next. Thus when Lazarsfeld and Menzel oppose the concept of a *structural* variable to those of *global* or analytical variable, the use of the word 'structure' is here intended to underline the distinction between the composition of 'structural variables'—which consist of relationships—and types of information other than relational. In this case, the synonymic association evoked may be summarized by the expression 'structure–system of relationships'. In effect, the variables involved serve to characterize a complex of components of elements as a system of relationships.

On the other hand, in the case of an opposition between structure and organization, the object is not to contrast something viewed as a system of relations with something regarded as an aggregate, but rather to distinguish between several systems of relations characteristic of an entity. In this case, the term structure is associated with the system of relations perceived as basic. Thus the association 'structure–system of relations' is subordinated to the association which can be summarized by the expression 'structure–essence'.

Since the meaning of the concept of structure varies with the context in which it is employed, it follows that one cannot provide a definition conveying its *content*. In other words, the concept of structure cannot be defined inductively in Lévi-Strauss's sense. Alternatively, in the context of intentional definitions, it is very difficult to provide a *paradigm* definition of 'structure'.[7] In an attempt to 'express' the content of this term, one is reduced to enumerating the associations and oppositions evoked, because (as has been shown) this concept, strictly speaking, has no other content. It is thus defined by its associations: 'structure–totality', 'structure–system of relationships', 'structure–whole irreducible to the sum of its parts', 'structure–essence', etc., as well as by the oppositions 'structure–outward appearance', 'structure–observable characteristics', 'structure–aggregate', 'structure–superficial system', etc.

However, the most illuminating definition of the term 'structure' in this type of context is the *constitutive* definition, which specifies its function: to recall the systematic character of an object or of an outlook, to distinguish between basic and outward systems of relationships, and so on.

As has already been said in the first chapter, the epistemologist endeavouring to find a general inductive definition for the concept of structure in the context of intentional definitions is comparable to the phonetician when he seeks to define a sound such as (*r*). If he tries to determine its objective characteristics by observing different pronunciations of this sound, he concludes that these are subject to considerable variations. Consequently, the sound (*r*) does not correspond to a set of well-defined characteristics. In objective terms, it has no identity. However, one cannot deny that all adult English speakers normally distinguish between words such as 'lice' and 'rice', or 'pain' and 'rain'. Hence it must be acknowledged that the sound or rather the phoneme (*r*) has an identity. The only method by which this contradiction can be resolved is through the recognition that the identity of a phoneme cannot be established inductively, and that such a definition is inappropriate.

The same is true of the concept 'structure', when used in the context of intentional definitions. Attempts to determine the common denominator of its different definitions are doomed to failure. Clearly these definitions vary enormously, and it would be impossible to explain either how the same word can be applied in so many different cases or how its meaning is universally understood when it appears in any given context. To resolve this difficulty, it is first necessary to admit that this method itself is inappropriate. The whole meaning of the term 'structure' in the context of intentional definitions is reducible to the paradigm and constitutional definitions mentioned earlier. From this angle, it does have a single meaning and an identity, despite the multiplicity of its applications.

One corollary of these propositions is that the debate surrounding such problems as whether the concept of 'social structure' should be distinguished from that of 'organization' or not, whether it should be assimilated to the concept of 'system of social relations', or whether inter-individual relationships should be included in the types of relationships characterizing social structures, is perfectly pointless and void, as experience has shown. The only relevant questions refer to the usefulness of distinguishing between an apparent system of relations and a real one. Since this distinction is indispensable in many cases, it is worth mentioning and convenient in practice to refer to it in an oppositional form 'structure/organization'. On the other hand, it is absurd to wonder what the right definition of the concept of 'social structure' is.

Similarly it is clear—to borrow an example from another field—that 'structural' or 'contextual' sociological surveys, which enable the construction of 'structural' or 'contextual' variables in Lazarsfeld's sense, represent a great methodological progress over atomistic surveys. Because the latter restrict themselves to enumerating individual characteristics,[8] they treat the individual as if he were detached from his environment, and hence as an abstraction. Structural surveys, on the other hand, make possible an analysis of the role 'social structures' play in individual behaviour, while the different types of 'social structures' are simultaneously determined. However, it would be absurd to ask if they are really capable of describing the structure of a social system, because this would involve the adoption of the *realistic* position which consists in postulating that systems—social or other—conceal a structure which one can seek to discover. All that can be said is that these 'structural' surveys produce information considerably richer in kind than do atomistic surveys. It is obvious—and will not be explained again—why the term 'structure' is used in connection with such surveys.

If one wishes to lift the debate to the philosophical plane, it appears that much of the confusion associated with the concept of structure derives from the fact that it carries overtones very close to the old philosophic concept of 'essence', to the extent that one tends to conceive of it in a realist manner. But the only way to grasp the meaning of the concept of structure is to understand that it appears within a scientific discourse and that it takes its meaning from the functions it performs within this particular discourse.

It will be seen in the following chapters that these propositions which have been sufficiently demonstrated for the concept of structure in the case of intentional definitions, are equally valid when this concept is associated with an effective definition. In such contexts, the word 'structure' is no more understandable in isolation from the logical procedures underpinning it than is the word 'hypothesis' in the experimental sciences if one ignores the basic procedures of these sciences.

From the first to the second type of context

Before moving on to the context of effective definitions of the term *structure*, it is perhaps useful to summarize the difference between the two types of contexts. One may wonder how it is possible to justify the use of the same word in contexts whose logical dualism appears irreducible.

To show that this dualism is not incompatible with a clear meaning and—in a certain way—a single meaning of the concept of structure, let us return to the example of Spearman. It is conceivable that the discovery of Spearman's unifactorial theory followed the stages that have been previously sketched: a matrix with a 'Spearman structure' is a matrix whose elements are linked by a certain number of relationships. Perhaps it was this fact which struck Spearman even before he had devised his theory. Similarly Guttman testifies that he himself was struck, when examining correlation matrices constructed from the results of psychometric tests, by the frequently observable fact that after rearranging the lines and the columns a decrease in the size of correlation coefficients occurs as one moves away from the main diagonal of the matrix (see the imaginary example below).

Tests	1	2	3	4	5
1		0·60	0·47	0·25	0·10
2	0·60		0·58	0·36	0·20
3	0·47	0·58		0·54	0·35
4	0·25	0·36	0·54		0·62
5	0·10	0·20	0·35	0·62	

In other words, in both the unifactorial matrix of Spearman and the 'simplex' matrix of Guttman, the first thing to attract the attention of these authors was that the elements composing the matrices which they were examining were inter-connected by a set of relationships. To express this statement in the language of the intentional definitions given to the concept of structure, it could be said that these matrices appeared as totalities of interdependent elements. They are thus *structures* in the meaning employed within the first type of contexts. Why is this so, why in other words is there order instead of a random distribution, and why this particular order rather than another? One is thus naturally led to produce a theory to account for it. The unifactorial theory of Spearman and the ordinal theory of Guttman are two examples of theories put forward to explain specific properties—structures (in the meaning employed within the first type of context)—of certain correlation matrices. But it must be noted that, from the moment a matrix is termed a 'unifactorial structure', a 'multifactorial structure' or a 'simplex structure', or given any other theoretical name, the concept of structure appears in the context of an operative definition.

In other cases, the research worker confronted with his specific data experiences a feeling analogous to that which has been attributed here to Spearman and to Guttman. He will have the feeling that the object investigated is a system, that the elements of this system are interdependent, that they have mutual relationships, and that it is impossible to understand them in isolation. He will summarize this impression by saying that the object investigated is a 'structure' or that it has a 'structure'. However, in the majority of cases it will be impossible for him to limit himself to this remark: he must go further to establish a theory accounting for this interdependence.

The above comments can be summed up by saying that it is indispensable in practice to recognize the duality of contexts in which the term structure appears, the two distinct types often representing two different periods in the analysis of a given subject. In the first stage, it appears that the subject-matter is not, to paraphrase Kroeber, 'completely amorphous', that it presents regularities, that its elements are interdependent, etc. In the second stage, theories are formulated to account for this interdependence: one thus passes from the first to the second type of context.

It would not be an exaggeration to state that the difficulties and ambiguities of the concept of structure are concentrated in the interval between these two stages. Thus, in the case of the psychometric matrices of Spearman and Guttman, the two stages coincide, or at least follow closely upon one another. The very idea of calculating the correlation coefficients between the tests already supposes a statistical backing. When it is subsequently observed that the results of certain groups of tests give rise to correlation matrices possessing particular 'structures' (in the meaning of the first type of context), the question naturally arises as to why this structure obtains in the given case. Attempts will then be made to formulate a theory. In other words, the fact that the question 'why this structure?' can be asked in this particular case implies that an answer to it can be given or, more precisely, that the methodology necessary to the elaboration of a reply is available.

However, this represents an exceptional case. In the majority of cases the two stages are separated, as the history of science shows, by years, decades or even centuries. One need go no further than to consider biology. Already Aristotle had the idea that the organism is a structure (in the meaning of the first type of context). But one had to wait until the twentieth century for this structure to be analysed by scientific theorists; until then, one had to be content with explaining the end to which living creatures tended by the metaphysical and tautological theory of final causes.[9]

Such considerations explain why it has been useful to term the first type of contexts *intentional*, since frequently the use of the word 'structure' in such contexts serves to describe an *intention*: the intention to construct or to present a theory analysing the interdependence of the elements of an object-system. However, it is equally common for such an intent not to lead to an *operative* implementation and to be incapable of such implementation, be it because the object itself does not permit it or because the necessary mental tools are not available. Hence the temptation—which explains the abuse of the word 'structure' in certain contexts—to use the word in a *magical* manner: in the absence of techniques to bring rain for crops, one can sing for rain, as some tribes do. Similarly certain structural analyses are only structural to the extent that they use the word structure as an incantation.

3

The Meaning of the Concept of Structure in the Context of Operative Definitions

THIS chapter deals with the case in which the word 'structure' appears in the context of an *operative* definition. As will be remembered from the example of factor analysis taken from Spearman in the preceding chapter, the concept of structure is associated in such a context with a logical construct. It is this construct which, when applied to an object-system, defines the 'structure' of this object. However, such a proposition is insufficient either to do away with or to explain the polysemic nature of the concept of structure in the second type of context. For this one must show—and *prima facie* it seems a hazardous undertaking—that such a definition of the concept of structure is equally applicable to cases as different as Spearman's factor analysis, the structural analysis of kinship, the structural analysis of social systems in Parsons' sense, or the analysis of social structure in the sense used by Murdock, to quote but a few examples.

This demonstration will be attempted by seeking to defend the view that while the structure of a system is always the result of a hypothetico-deductive theory applied to the given system, certain *constraints*—imposed by the specific nature of the material examined—mean that these theories can take extremely diverse forms. This will involve in some cases a mathematical model susceptible of verification, in others a group of verbal propositions whose inferences will be arrived at by a rough deductive procedure akin to that of a syllogism. Furthermore, in some cases the theory may be associated with a verificatory criterion of an unambiguous nature, while in others it will be impossible to relate a theory to a criterion of this kind. In the latter, one will have to be content with the degree of subjective certitude engendered by the theory. Finally, in certain cases the system analysed is borrowed directly from nature, while in others it is constructed by the research-worker himself. However, before proceeding to this demonstration, which will be undertaken by means of a detailed analysis of certain precise examples of 'structure', several preliminary remarks are in order.

Generally the distinction between the context of intentional definitions and that of operative ones can be reduced to a difference between the two types of definition. In the former, the concept of structure is always associated, implicitly or explicitly, with an enumeration of characteristics allowing, at least in principle, the identification of the type of object which one wishes to designate by the noun 'structure' or by the adjective 'structural', etc. To cite again as an example of this kind of context the definition given by Flament [15], 'a structure is a group of elements connected by relationships, such that any modification of one element or one relationship modifies other elements or relationships'. A definition whose *contents* are obviously different, but whose logical *type* is identical, can be borrowed from Katona [23]. In effect, with this author the concept of structure is related to the idea that 'all items or parts (of a structure) are influenced by the whole to which they belong'. However, Katona adds, in order to make his thought more explicit, that the whole being different from the sum of its parts 'does not necessarily mean that the whole is more than the sum of its parts'. Indeed 'the change in one item or part may or may not affect the whole or the other items and parts, depending on the role and function of the part within the whole' (p. 32). The two definitions presented above—and chosen from among thousands—differ in their contents. For Flament, change in one element necessarily involves modification of the whole. For Katona, such an effect is left conditional. Nevertheless the two definitions belong to the same logical type. This type involves the enumeration of specific characteristics that enable an object to be identified as a 'structure'. In other words, the type of definition used is a *definition by difference*.

The same type of definition can be detected whenever the concept of structure—without being the object of a formal

E

definition as in the examples quoted—is used because it evokes
the synonymic associations 'structure–whole', 'structure–system
of relationships', etc. As has been seen in the preceding
chapter, concepts like 'structural effect' (Blau), or 'structural
variable' (Lazarsfeld and Menzel) should be added to this
category. In opposition to definitions by difference, which
characterize the examples given in that chapter, the definitions
that have been termed *operative* are definitions by *construction*.
Here the concept of structure is neither implicitly nor explicitly
the object of the definition based on a list of specific characteristics. Instead, definition depends upon a construct by which the
'structure' of an object-system is determined.

This distinction can be likened to that between the classical
theory of definition by *genus proximum* and *differentia specifica* on
the one hand and the mathematical concept of definition by
construction[1] on the other. To clarify this comparison, it can be
said that when the concept of structure is defined by Flament or
Katona, they engage in a mental operation analogous to that
undertaken by the naturalist when he defines the concept of
'dog': this involves associating with the given concept a certain
number of attributes which enable one to distinguish it from
the concepts of, for example, 'horse' or 'flower'. By contrast,
the psychologist who defines the concept of 'factorial structure'
proceeds rather like the mathematician defining the concept of
an integer. In such a case no attempt is made to define the
concept of 'integer' by distinguishing it from other concepts.
The definition actually coincides with the description of the
procedure whereby a new number can be obtained from one
already arrived at: 2 will thus be defined by the expression
$2 = 1 + 1$; 3 by the expression $3 = 2 + 1$, etc.

Thus the definition of the concept of structure in a case such
as Spearman's factor analysis does correspond to a definition
by construction. The expression 'factorial structure' is incomprehensible in isolation from the logical construct with which it
is associated, but it becomes unambiguous as soon as the construct has been understood.

In concluding these preliminary remarks it might be worth
while to dispose of a possible objection to the distinction between
the context of intentional definitions and that of operative

definitions. The point could have been made that instead of distinguishing between these two types of definitions an alternative approach would be to state that the first context corresponds to the case in which a general definition of the concept of structure is aimed at, whereas the second corresponds to that of an attempted description of an object-system, be it the system of marriage rules in a given society or the system of answers to a battery of psychometric tests.

The first answer to this objection is that the concept of structure may appear in the context of an intentional definition and yet be associated with a category of very specific objects. Thus the concept of 'structural effect' (Blau) only makes sense in the very specific situation in which a number of individual variables and of collective variables are defined. In this sense it is no more general than Spearman's concept of structure. Secondly, when one mentions the 'structure' of an object-system in the context of an operative definition, one is bound to refer to a general image of the concept of structure. In other words, since the term 'structure' is used in the two types of contexts about very different objects, this term must have or must be thought to have an identity throughout these specific contexts. Hence it is impossible to differentiate in this respect between the two types of contexts.

To analyse the meaning of the concept of structure in the context of operative definitions poses the same problem as does the corresponding analysis in the context of intentional definitions. The aim in both cases is to explain the feeling that one is dealing with homonyms when expressions such as 'structure', 'structural', 'structural analysis', etc. are associated with constructs that are obviously different from each other. One may well wonder in what respects the constructs associated with the concept of 'social structure' by Murdock, Parsons and Lévi-Strauss are comparable. How is one then to justify the fact that the heterogeneous analytical tools used by sociologists, psychologists, economists, phonologists or grammarians are all labelled 'structuralism'? Similarly, how can the concept of structure have a meaning if it designates indiscriminately methods which appear unrelated?

As in the contexts analysed in the previous chapter, the contradiction between the feeling that the concept of structure has an identity and the undeniable variety of its applications must be elucidated. To resolve this problem, it is first necessary to examine a sample of contexts related to an *operative* definition of the concept of structure. An attempt has been made to choose these examples from the greatest possible range of disciplines and to select those cases where the concept of structure is clearly associated with a variety of constructs.

The sources of homonymy in the context of operative definitions

As was announced in the first chapter, the thesis advanced here will be the following: to be able to speak of structure in this type of context, it is first necessary to conceive the object to be analysed as a *system*. In other words, it must be conceived of as a whole made up of interdependent elements. Several examples are now given to clarify this concept of *system*.

1. Let us imagine a group of specific elements, like the marriage rules of a given society. This *group* becomes a system as soon as the principle is put forward that these rules cannot be analysed except in relation to one another. To view these rules as a system excludes the possibility of their being interpreted, for example, as the product of a series of historical contingencies.

2. Let us take another group of elements, such as the rules governing stress in a given language. Here again it is possible to view these rules as simple facts, which only require recording. They are seen as a system as soon as the principle is put forward that they have mutual implications and that each of them is indispensable to the understanding of others.

3. Another example of *system* is provided by the two fictitious psychometric matrices presented on pages 22 and 49. These two tables both contain a group of elements related to one another. Thus in the matrix on page 22, as soon as the mathematical relationships involved are known (those analysed on pages 23–27), it is possible, knowing one item in column i and the corresponding item in column j, to fill the two columns.

It should be noted at this point that these hypotheses— which tend to consider the object analysed as a *system*—do not necessarily exclude other hypotheses. In effect, there is nothing to prevent historical investigations into an institution, or a given marriage rule, or the evolution of a rule of stress in language. In this case, the group of institutions, marriage rules or stress conventions are clearly not considered as systems. In other cases, the interpretation of a group as a *system* is obligatory. This is so in the case of the correlation matrices constructed from the results of psychometric tests presented earlier. It can thus be said that, except in particular cases, there is no necessity in principle to consider an object as a system. All that should be underlined is that the concept of 'structure' does not apply until it is decided to consider a given object as a system.

This hypothesis having been stated, it is now necessary to show that the object is in fact a system. To put it more precisely, it must be demonstrated that the elements of a group which is considered as a system are really interdependent. In other words, the interdependence between these component elements must be analysed. The result of this analysis is what could be termed a 'systems theory'. The description or interpretation of the object-system resulting from this theory is nothing other than the *structure* of this object. It is that which defines the concepts of *structure* in this type of context.

This we hold to be the only possible definition of the concept of structure in the context of effective definitions. It is closely related to the concept of 'systems theory'. The purpose of this study will be to demonstrate that in all cases in which the concept appears in this type of context, it is related to a theory concerning an object considered as a system.

This said, it remains to present a theory of the *homonymic* character of the concept of structure in this type of context. If the statements made above define the concept of structure in the context of operative definitions, it is still necessary to explain how the 'structural analyses' found in scientific literature can be so diverse in their degree of rigour and in the conviction they carry.

In the contexts examined in the previous chapter, the sources of homonymy were readily identifiable. It has been seen that these sources result from the fact that the concept of structure often appears in opposition to other terms, and generally in

specific contexts which evoke one or another particular synonymic association.

Here the feeling of homonymy is also an effect of the types
of environment in which the concept of structure appears.
More exactly, two principal sources of homonymy can be
distinguished.

The first source of homonymy

Firstly, the 'theories' associated with the concept of structure
in any given case can be of different logical types.

1. In certain cases, these theories represent testable hypothetico-deductive systems. They have the logical form of a set
of propositions or *axioms* from which it is possible by deduction
to obtain new propositions or *inferences*. The system of propositions thus formed is testable to the extent that certain of these
inferences, or sometimes all of them, can be compared with the
properties of the object analysed. Spearman's factor theory is
an example conforming to this type. In effect, the procedure
consists primarily in formulating the hypothesis that the results
obtained from a given population taking a group of tests are
coherent. More precisely, it is assumed that they can be explained
by one general factor and by several subordinate ones, whose
effects are independent from one test to another. This hypothesis
can thus be translated into formal terms. The success of one
subject at a test is explained as a linear function of a general
factor and of specific factors (first axiom set). Secondly, a
certain number of measurement conventions are introduced
(second axiom set). Finally, the concepts of *general factor* and
specific factors are interpreted in the light of the assumption
that they are statistically independent (third axiom set). Taken
together, these axioms constitute a hypothetico-deductive
system, from which a theorem is deduced whereby the correlation coefficients between the tests should be associated by
relationships of the form $r_{ij}/r_{ik} = r_{mj}/r_{mk}$, where $i, j, k,$ and m
designate four tests.

In order to ascertain whether this theory adequately describes the assumed coherence of results, one must first check
whether these relationships are satisfactory when the empirically

obtained correlation coefficients between scores measuring performance on different tests are inspected. If they are, the theory can be considered as an adequate representation of the system of scores. If this does not obtain, the theory must be rejected. However, it is important in the latter case to check whether the theory was actually constructed in a manner capable of testing by the application of a simple criterion.

In the following it will be shown that a great number of the theories associated with 'structural' analysis of an object-system are of this type.

2. In other cases, the theory remains a hypothetico-deductive system, but it cannot be tested by the application of a simple and unambiguous criterion. However, this testing cannot be termed impossible. Indeed the theory may be compatible with a great number of events without this compatibility constituting a criterion of testability as strict as in the previous case. Let us take for example the case of Jakobson's phonology. As the outcome of a complicated process, he identified a certain number of phonemes in the English language which he described by reference to a group of 'distinctive traits'. Thus the phoneme i as it appears in the word 'pit' is described as 'vocalic', 'non-consonantal', 'diffuse', 'acute', whereas the phoneme h as it appears in the word 'hill' is described as 'non-vocalic', 'non-consonantal', 'drawn-out', and the phoneme $\#$, which represents silence, as 'non-vocalic', 'non-consonantal', 'loose'. The unexpected character of these descriptions shows clearly that they result from a theory. Be that as it may, the description of phonemes deriving from this theory permits their classification according to a certain order of complexity. It is claimed that this order of complexity roughly coincides with the dropping of phonemes by aphasics, and also with the order of phoneme-learning by children. The relationship between the order of phonemes obtained from the theory and these empirical orderings is clearly a test that confirms the theory itself. In other words, one has a greater tendency to feel confidence in this theory when one is aware of its coincidence with these other orderings. However, strictly speaking it cannot be said that they constitute a proof of validity for the theory. Neither could

it be said that an absence of association between the theoretical and the empirical orders would constitute an unequivocal refutation for the theory. In brief, absence of association could not in this case represents a criterion of falsification. This derives from the fact that the theory from which the description of phonemes is drawn enables one to deduce the order of complexity of phonemes, but not a necessary coincidence between this order and, for example, the usage of phonemes by children. It is for this reason that an absence of coincidence cannot be considered as falsifying the theory. In a case of this kind, it would be said that the theory is associated with *indirect* testing procedures. It will later be seen that most of the work carried out under the label of structural phonology and associated with the names of Jakobson, Troubetzkoi, Harris and others is of this type.[2]

3. In other cases still, the theory is a hypothetico-deductive system, but it is strictly speaking impossible to define either direct or indirect criteria for testability. Such a theory by rather complex processes may evoke a variable degree of conviction and thus be judged as more or less *likely*. However, the theory is not properly testable either directly or indirectly. For example, this is illustrated by the psycho-analytical theory about personality structure. It thus appears that the concept of structure has an identity—to the extent that it is always associated with a theory which seeks to explain or interpret the *systematic* nature of an object—while nevertheless giving rise to a strong feeling of homonymy. It would be too complex to investigate here why systems analysis is sometimes related to a testable theory, while at other times it is associated with a theory which simply seems likely.[3]

The second source of homonymy

Apart from this first source, a second one can be cited. The object-systems to which 'structural' analysis is applied can differ substantively.

In all cases and by definition, these objects are, or more exactly *are conceived of* as systems, that is to say—once again—as objects which can be analysed as made up of interdependent elements. However, these systems can differ considerably in terms of the difficulties preventing their observation. Some are made up of a group of facts, characteristics or components, which are easy to detect and whose number is well defined. In such a case it can be said that one is dealing with *well-defined systems*. Others, by contrast, are made up of components which cannot always be identified with certainty and whose number is indefinite. In such a case it can be said that one is dealing with *undefined systems*. To illustrate this distinction, let us take a number of examples.

In the analysis of 'kinship structures', the system dealt with concerns the marriage rules of a given society. The aim is to explain how these rules make up a coherent whole from inter-dependent elements. In this case, the system analysed is comprised of the complete set of marriage rules. These rules can be easily detected and formulated. Furthermore, their number is finite. Thus one knows that in Tarau society all marriage between first cousins is forbidden, with the exception of marriage with the daughter of the mother's brother. Hence one is dealing with a *well-defined* system.

Some research in the sphere of structural syntax—which has already been alluded to and which will be examined in greater detail later—has tried to show that stress in a given language forms coherent patterns whose system of fundamental rules can be deduced. Such research has concentrated upon the investigation of the stress phenomenon in the English language. In this case, the systems which are analysed are the stress phenomena attached to such and such phrases or such and such a sentence in the English language. Thus, when an English-speaker voices a phrase such as 'John's blackboard eraser', he associates with each of these syllables a stress of a given relative intensity. According to phoneticians, the stress is most pro-nounced on the syllable 'black' in this phrase; 'John's' carries a slightly weaker intensity of stress; the 'a' of 'eraser' has an even weaker stress; while the syllable least stressed is 'board'. In cases like this the systems analysed are thus easily detectable sets of components, whose number is finite. In the case of stress in the phrase 'John's blackboard eraser', the set of phenomena characteristic of the system is the hierarchy of four degrees of stress. One is thus dealing once again with a well-defined system.

Let us now examine an intermediate case: that of an undefined system which is arbitrarily transformed into a well-defined one. Consider for example the situation where Spearman's factorial analysis is applied to a set of psychometric tests. Obviously a finite number of tests is always administered to a given population. Consequently the system to be analysed, represented by the correlation matrix between the tests, is composed of a set of elements, perfectly defined and detectable, which are no other than the correlation coefficients themselves.

However, this situation is logically different from that in the preceding cases. In fact the 'choice' of elements retained is arbitrary.[4] In other words, the system constituted by the correlation matrix between the scores is *well defined*. But this is due to the fact of a prior arbitrary decision. Ultimately the marriage rules of a society or the phenomena of stress in a spoken phrase constitute systems that could be termed *naturally defined*.

Finally, there are cases—and very numerous at that—of systems naturally undefined which it is difficult to reduce to well-defined systems. Thus it is clear—as has been known since Montesquieu—that among the institutions or the values of a society certain of them constitute systems or sets of interdependent elements. This said, it is obvious that 'social systems' are systems naturally undefined which are difficult to reduce to well-defined ones by arbitrary decisions. The same holds when one speaks, as is done currently in psychology, of 'personality structure'. In this case, one refers to an object whose characteristics are those of an undefined system. These distinctions are too obvious to labour.

Although they are obvious, it appears that their relevance for analysing the apparently polysemic character of the concept of structure has not been sufficiently noted. Yet it is almost self-evident that the concept of structure must have a different echo according to its association with a well-defined system or with an undefined system. Similarly, the virtues of 'structural analysis' must vary considerably between the case in which a testable hypothetico-deductive theory has been constructed and that in which the theory is merely 'likely'. On the other hand, a *testable* theory applied to a *well-defined* system ought to be more convincing than a likely theory applied to an undefined system. Hence one naturally considers as homonymous the meaning which Lévi-Strauss gives to the concept of structure when he speaks of 'kinship structures' and that which Parsons gives to the expression 'social structure'. Moreover the concept of structure in these two cases is associated with a theoretical interpretation given to the systematic character of the object considered.

A pessimistic corollary of this discussion should be noted in passing: if the analysis given is acceptable, it follows that the success of what have been generically termed 'structural methods' depends upon the characteristics of the object considered. In certain cases these methods lead to theories whose rigour is comparable to those of the natural sciences. In others, the theories involved seem to persuade rather than convince. Indeed the problem does not rest in giving an object the status of 'system' and in considering it within a 'structuralist' perspective. Other conditions must be met. Thus before a testable theory can be applied to this object, the latter must be adequately delineated.

The foregoing can be summarized by saying—at the risk of shocking devotees of ill-defined structuralism—that the 'structuralist' perspective has no intrinsic virtue. The success met with in its application depends to a large extent upon the object analysed. Naturally it is also necessary to have the formal tools available that are required for theory formation.

If the two distinctions just presented are reduced to dichotomies—distinction between the types of object-systems, on the one hand, and between the types of theories associated with structural analysis, on the other—one obtains four types of structures (Table 1).

Table I. *The four main types of setting of the concept of structure in the context of operative definitions*

	Well-defined object-system	Undefined object-system
Testable theory	Type 1	Type 2
Indirectly testable theory or untestable theory	Type 3	Type 4

It is difficult to demonstrate that the two dimensions summarized by this table—as well as the types of structure that are derived from it—exhaustively analyse the environments of the concept of structure. In conjunction with the examples that follow it is hoped to show that these distinctions are fundamental. One will see that these examples belonging to each of the four types give rise to a feeling of synonymy, while examples from different types give rise to homonymy. The concept of structure appears unambiguously defined within each of these types. Two examples taken from different types give rise to a feeling of homonymy. As has been understood, the problem posed by the meaning of the concept of structure in the context of *operative* definitions involves a demonstration of the identity of this concept above the differences due to its particular logical setting.

In the present chapter, we will examine several examples belonging to types 1 and 2.

First example of type I: structure analysis of stress in English.
The first example examined is the structural analysis of stress in English, contributed by Chomsky and Miller [8], [9], [41].

This theory of stress in English is part of a series of research studies conducted by Chomsky and Miller on grammar in natural languages. The basic hypothesis of their work is that grammatical rules are not arbitrary conventions, but systems which permit the decoding or the comprehension of an unequivocal message. They have attempted to show that the syntactic properties of sentences or phrases accepted in a language as grammatically correct may be deduced from a system of very general rules, so that the formation of a grammatically correct message may be envisaged as the product of a deduction from these general rules. This work is still at a preliminary stage. However, as the following brief analysis of stress in English will show, it is both revolutionary and promising.

It is a commonplace to view rules of stress in English as a sum of arbitrary rules—an *aggregate*. The difficulties experienced by foreigners learning these rules provide corroborative evidence. Yet, while it is true that such rules consist merely in a small number of general principles qualified by manifold exceptions, how does one account for the fact that a normal adult whose mother tongue is English can use them confidently and that a child learns them rapidly? The question, though obviously pertaining to the field of linguistics, links up with the psychological problems of learning and of language use.

The only way to overcome the contradiction contained in these remarks is to show that the rules of stress do form, in spite of appearances, a whole—*a system*—which is coherent, and that most special cases derive in fact from general rules.

At first, this statement seems foolhardy. It is difficult to view as anything but accidental the fact that two words as close to each other as 'compensation' and 'condensation', for example, are pronounced quite differently. In 'compensation', the vowel "e" is *reduced* and the word is pronounced 'comp'nsation'. By contrast, in 'condensation', although stress is in the same place as in 'compensation', the vowel "e" is slightly audible. To borrow another example from Chomsky and Miller, how does one account for the marked variation which occurs in the pronunciation of the segment 'telegraph' according to context? In 'telegraph' and 'telegraphic', the vowel in the second syllable is 'reduced'. By contrast, it is distinctly audible in 'telegraphy'. Furthermore, whereas the first and last syllables of 'telegraph' are equally stressed,* the corresponding syllables of 'telegraphic' are not, the first one being less stressed than the third. Obviously it is difficult at the start to view these rules as anything other than arbitrary conventions. However, if they were arbitrary, how could one account for the ease with which they are learnt and the confidence with which they are applied?

Moreover some examples confirm that these rules must be seen as a coherent system. Indeed in certain cases they perform an important function: that of making a message unambiguous. Thus, if context is disregarded, the written expression 'small boys' school' may mean both 'a school for little boys' and 'a small school for boys'. But it becomes unambiguous in the spoken language, since the phrase 'small boys' school' is stressed 'small^3 boys^1 school^3' when it has the first meaning and

*According to Chomsky and Miller!

'small boys' school' in the latter case. The figures located above the words show the extent to which these are stressed.

Contrary to previous theory, these examples induce the impression that the rules of stress make up a coherent system, or at any rate that they perform important functions in speech.

Chomsky and Miller's work shows that the rules of stress in English may be considered as derived from a limited number of general principles or axioms. More precisely they make the point that the hope to arrive one day at a theory which would permit deductions about the stress of any segment in the English language is not an unreasonable one. In particular, it is possible to show that the peculiarities mentioned earlier, for instance the difference between the pronunciation of 'compensation' and that of 'condensation' are inferences correctly drawn from these principles. Apart from enabling one to account for specific facts, the principles in question provide, at least in theory, the means of reconstituting the stress of almost any segment in the English language. This will be substantiated by Chomsky's analysis of the expression 'John's blackboard eraser', which has already been quoted and whose stress can be summarized as follows: 'John's blackboard eraser'.

An understanding of the Chomsky–Miller theory requires one to have adequately grasped the concept of 'structural description' of a segment. Let us take an elementary example, that of the expression 'small boys' school'. When it means 'a small school for boys', the two words 'boys' school' constitute, to use rather imprecise terms, a unit within the wider unit made up by the whole expression. Such an analysis can be summed up by a system of brackets, the expression being represented as follows: ['small (boys' school)']. Similarly, if the phrase means 'a school for little boys', it will be transcribed as ['(small boys') school'].

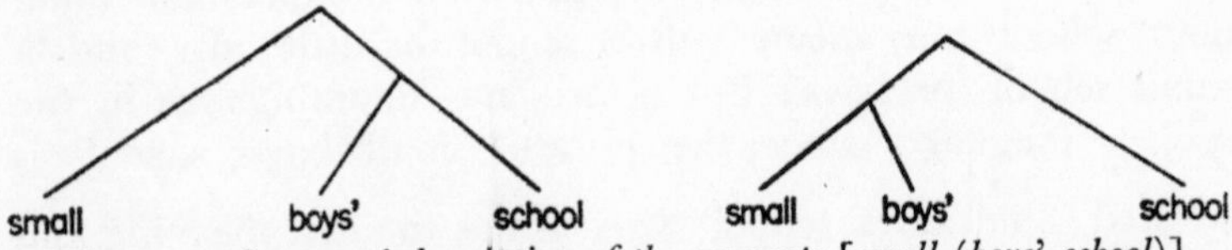

Figure 4: Structural description of the segments [small (boys' school)] and [(small boys') school] by means of logical trees

An equivalent representation by means of logical trees enables one to distinguish between the structure of these two segments, as in figure 4. The part played by brackets in the previous representation is performed here by the *tops* of the tree. Similarly, when a set of brackets is included within another, the top corresponding to the first is *dominated* by that corresponding to the second. A logical identity exists therefore between the two methods of presentation.

In order to account for the syntax of both expressions, the systems of hierarchically defined brackets must clearly be *classified*. Indeed, in [(small boys') school], the parentheses '(...)' separate a component part of the 'compound word' represented by the expression as a whole. By contrast, in [small (boys' school)], the parentheses '(...)' separate a compound within an expression which is not itself a compound word. A way of expressing these distinctions consists in classifying the system of brackets at various levels by reference to the grammatical nature of the components they contain. Naturally this procedure cannot be described in detail here; it will suffice to understand the principle involved.

Briefly and schematically, it can be said that the structural description of an expression consists in: (1) analysing this expression with a view to discovering its component parts; (2) associating these components with a hierarchy of systems of brackets; (3) classifying these systems. If the representation by means of logical trees is preferred, it will suffice to say that a tree must be associated with every segment and that the tops of this tree must be classified. Thus the structural description of the message 'small boys' school' ('a small school for boys') will be: $[_B$small $(_A$boys' school$)]$ $_A]_B$. However, when the message means 'a school for little boys', it will be associated with the structural expression $[_A$ $(_A$small boys'$)_A$school$]_A$.

The general rules that enable one to deduce all the facts about stress connected with the examples selected[5] can now be formulated.

Rule a—This is a *de facto* rule, valid under very general conditions. It is formulated as follows: a simple or compound noun is generally stressed in an initial position.

Rule b—This is called 'the adjustment of stress'. Let us assume that an expression such as 'John's blackboard eraser' has been split up into three components, in the following way: {John's [(blackboard) eraser)]}. In this example, [(blackboard) eraser] is a compound word. Hence the parentheses '(...)', which separate the component 'blackboard', and the square brackets '[...]', which separate the component 'blackboard eraser', may be classified as belonging to the same category, which will be arbitrarily designated by index A. Thus one will write: $[_A(_A$ blackboard) $_A$ eraser$]_A$.

In such a case, rule b states that when two systems of brackets included one within the other and belonging to the same category are observed, the first main stress *is* dominant and lowers the others by one degree. Let us take the expression $[_A$ ($_A$ blackboard)$_A$ eraser$]_A$. By virtue of rule a, the component ($_A$ blackboard)$_A$ is stressed in an initial position. As for the term 'eraser', the stress is on the 'a'. Therefore the following stress may provisionally be associated with this expression: $[_A$ ($_A$ $\overset{1}{\text{black}}$ $\overset{2}{\text{board}}$) $_A$ $\overset{1}{\text{eraser}}]_A$. But, by virtue of rule b, the stress on 'black' is dominant and lowers the other stresses by one degree. Hence the stress $[_A$ $\overset{1}{\text{black}}$ $\overset{3}{\text{board}}$ $\overset{2}{\text{eraser}}]_A$.

Rule c—A new rule must be introduced in order to restore the stress corresponding to the whole expression 'John's blackboard eraser'. For, while the brackets containing, on the one hand, 'blackboard' and, on the other, 'blackboard eraser' belong to the same type (type A), the braces {...} cannot be considered as belonging to the same type as the square brackets '[...]'. The expression as a whole is not a compound noun. Rule b can therefore not be applied with a view to deleting the square brackets. Without going into details, it will suffice to associate with the expression as a whole the structural representation: $\{_B$ John's $[_A$ ($_A$ blackboard)$_A$ eraser$]$ $_A\}$ $_B$. Rule c, in stylized form, states that, when several main stresses have been defined within the systems of brackets belonging to different types, the last main stress is dominant and lowers the others by one degree.

To revert to the same example, the following provisional stress was recorded before deleting the square brackets:

$\{_B$ John's $[_A$ black board eraser$]$ $_A\}_B$. However, by applying rule c, one can delete the square brackets and arrive at the stress of the expression as a whole, provided all stresses are lowered by one degree to the exclusion of the *last* main stress.

Ultimately stress thus reads: $(_B$ John's black board eraser$)_B$.

This last expression describes stress as an English-speaker would place it in this phrase.

Obviously the rules which have just been formulated would be of little use if they enabled one to analyse only the stress on 'John's blackboard eraser'. Their interest derives from their ability to account for very diverse cases of stress.

For example, the message 'small boys' school', when it means 'a school for little boys', is stressed as follows: (small boys' school). When it means 'a small school for boys', it is stressed as follows: (small boys' school). It is easy to see that these facts result from the rules which have just been outlined.

Let us begin with the case in which the expression means 'a school for little boys' and is therefore associated with the structural description $[_A (_A$ small boys'$)$ $_A$ school$]_A$. In such a case, by applying rule c to 'small boys', the first transformation 'cycle' leads to the provisional stress: $[_A (_A$ small boys'$)_A$ school$]_A$. Indeed the structural description of 'small boys' may be considered as belonging to the type $[_B$ small $(_A$ (boys$)_A]_B$. Structurally the expression 'small boys' is of the same type as the expression $\{_B$ John's $[_A$ blackboard eraser$]$ $_A\}_B$.

Then, by applying rules a and b, the second transformation cycle is arrived at, i.e. $(_A$ small boys' school$)_A$. Indeed since segment $(_A \ldots)_A$ is a compound noun, it is the first stress of an intensity equal to 1 which is dominant. By virtue of rule b, it lowers other stresses by one degree.

Finally, by applying a general rule which will not be explained here, one arrives at the last cycle, which restores the common stress: (small boys' school).

In the case in which the same expression means 'a small school for boys', the associated structural description may be schematized as follows $[_B$ small $(_A$ boys' school $_A)]_B$. By applying

F

rule *a* to the component 'boys' school', the first transformation cycle is arrived at: $[_B$ sm$\overset{1}{\text{a}}$ll $(_A$ b$\overset{1}{\text{o}}$ys' sch$\overset{2}{\text{oo}}$l$)_A]$ $_B$. Since the expression $(_A\ldots)_A$ is a compound noun, it is stressed in an initial position. As the two systems of brackets are of different types, this being shown by their respective indices, the brackets may be deleted by applying rule *c*. Thus the second transformation cycle leads to the stress: $[_B$ sm$\overset{2}{\text{a}}$ll b$\overset{1}{\text{o}}$ys' sch$\overset{3}{\text{oo}}$l$]$ $_B$, which corresponds to the stress placed in fact by an English-speaker: (sm$\overset{2}{\text{a}}$ll b$\overset{1}{\text{o}}$ys' sch$\overset{3}{\text{oo}}$l).

In order to show the general applicability of the Chomsky–Miller theory, several other examples will be examined, after introducing a fourth general rule concerning the phenomenon of 'vowel reduction', to which reference has already been made.

Rule d—A vowel is reduced if no main stress has ever been placed on it in the course of any transformation cycle, or if the successive transformation cycles reduced the main stress placed upon it to a stress of the *third* order, and in some cases of the *second*.

Added to previous ones, this rule enables one to analyse, for example, the apparently incomprehensible difference in the pronunciation of words such as 'compensation' and 'condensation' or 'torrent' and 'torment'. The first word in each of these couples is characterized by a reduction of the vowel 'e', whereas this same vowel is distinctly audible in 'condensation' and in 'torment'.

For example, let us analyse the word 'condensation' by reference to the principles which have been outlined above. As there is a verb 'to condense', this word can be considered as the synthesis of two components: 'condens'- and '-ation'. Without going into the details of the analysis involved, the structure of the word 'condensation' may be represented in accordance with the principles previously used to describe the structure, not of words, but of sets of words. Thus the description $[_B\,(_A$ condens$)\,_A$ation$]$ $_B$ will be associated with 'condensation'.

The verb 'condense' is accentuated on the second syllable. The first transformation cycle is therefore: $[_B\,(_A$ condens$)_A$ ation$]$ $_B$.

However, by applying rule c, the brackets may be deleted, provided all the stresses are reduced by one degree, except the last one. Hence the pronunciation: ($_B$ $\overset{3\ \ 2\ \ 1}{\text{condensation}}$)$_B$. By virtue of rule d, the vowel 'e' is not reduced, since a main stress was placed upon it and was not reduced to the third degree.

By contrast, the word 'compensation' does not derive from a verb such as 'compense'. Therefore it cannot be split up and must be associated with the structural description ($_A$ compensation)$_A$. The final stress is thus arrived at by a single transformation cycle, which corresponds to the application of the familiar rule whereby the main stress on words ending in '-ation' is placed on this termination. This single cycle is represented as follows: ($_A$ $\overset{1}{\text{compensation}}$)$_A$. However, by virtue of rule d, the vowel 'e' is *reduced* if it has not had in any transformation cycle the main stress (of intensity 1) placed upon it. Thus the apparently strange difference in pronouncing 'condensation' and 'compensation' is accounted for. It is not a case of applying a general rule to one word, and making an exception for the other; the pronunciation of both is in fact deduced from general rules.

These comments, it is hoped, give a sufficiently clear insight into the structural theory of stress in English to allow for the use of this theory as an example. It is by reference to this example that the meaning of the concept of structure in the type of context discussed will be analysed.

To consider the object of the analysis first, one can see that it is facts of stress associated with any spoken segment of the English language that are dealt with. In theory, the purpose is therefore to account for the stress in any segment in English. In practice, however, it is obviously impossible to test whether the theories account for *all* facts of stress. Some such facts, which correspond to segments never pronounced until now, cannot by definition be observed. It will therefore suffice to ascertain that it accounts for a number of facts large enough to carry conviction.

Having formulated this reservation, one can consider that the small unit of speech previously designated as 'a segment' is the elementary object of the analysis. In other words, while it is true that a theory of stress should, at least in principle, account for all possible segments, yet each specific analysis deals with one given segment. Such a segment may consist of a sentence ('they are cooking apples'), a phrase ('John's blackboard eraser') or a word ('compensation'). For the theory to cover it, one only has to be able to distinguish in it a set of facts of stress viewed as interdependent.

Hence the object of the analysis is a system; and moreover it is a well-defined one. Thus, in the expression 'small boys' school', the system is made up of three facts of stress summarized by the representation (small boys' school).

All the facts which define a system will from now on be referred to as its *apparent characteristics*.

The 'structural analysis' conducted by Chomsky and Miller consists in a system of propositions or axioms from which it is possible to obtain by *calculation*[6] the *apparent characteristics* of any elementary system. It should be remembered that this is only a definition in principle and that, in practice, one will be content to ascertain that the main propositions make it possible to deduce rules of stress for as large a number of segments as possible, not for all of them.

To be more precise, let us designate by S a system, such as, for example, the word 'compensation' or the expression 'John's blackboard eraser', etc., and by A the system of axioms or the *axioms set* of which the four rules analysed above are a sample. Let us represent the structural description of a system S by the symbol $Str(S)$. In the case of the expression 'John's blackboard eraser', this structural description is represented by the expression $\{_B \text{John's} [_A (_A \text{blackboard})_A \text{eraser}]_A\}_B$. Lastly the apparent characteristics of system S will be designated by $App(S)$. In the case of the example used, $App(S)$ is represented by the expression (John's blackboard eraser). In other words, $App(S)$ sums up the four propositions: 'In the expression within braces, the stress on *John's* is of an intensity equal to 2, the main stress on *black* of an intensity equal to 1, etc.' It can then be said that the conjunction of A and $Str(S)$ defines a *calculation*.

As has already been seen, the stages of this calculation correspond to a series of transformation cycles which enable one to successively delete the brackets associated with the structural description by applying the rules of A. The results of the calculation defined by A and $Str(S)$ coincide precisely with $App(S)$. In other words, the whole set of apparent characteristics pertaining to system S is obtained by deduction from A and from $Str(S)$.

To sum up, one can write:

$$(1) \qquad\qquad A + Str(S) \xrightarrow{\text{Calculation}} App(S)$$

Several comments may be made in connection with this formula.

First, it should be noted that A is implicitly defined by Chomsky and Miller, so that formula (1) be verified whatever S may be. In other words, the axioms A and the structural description $Str(S)$ of any segment S being given, A and $Str(S)$ must define a calculation which makes it possible to deduce the apparent characteristics of a system, i.e. $App(S)$.

On the other hand, the structure $Str(S)$ of a system S is relative to A. The very formulation of the axioms contained in A implies that the structural description $Str(S)$ should comply with a number of formal rules. In other words, the syntax of A implies that $Str(S)$ must in turn comply with a given syntax. In particular, one sees that the structural description must analyse a system in the form of a set of classified components so that the rules of A are applicable. One cannot *calculate* the apparent characteristics of system S unless the structural description of S is formulated in an appropriate language. It must be clearly stated that the structure of a segment, symbolized by $Str(S)$, is such only in relation to A. Hence one cannot consider a structural description like $\{_B$ John's $[_A (_A$ blackboard$)$ $_A\}$ $_B$ as representing the 'structure' of this expression in an absolute sense or, if one prefers to put it otherwise, as conveying the essence of this expression. One can only say that such a structural description, when associated with axiom set A, enables one to reproduce exactly the effective stress on this segment. Of course this does not mean that any theory—i.e. any set composed of $A + Str(S)$—is equally acceptable. Indeed it is abundantly clear that if the whole collection of segments explained by theory T_1 is comprised within the set of segments explained by theory T_2, the latter theory will be preferred, as being more general. Furthermore, several sets, such as $App(S)$, may be associated with a system S. Let us take for example the sentence: 'they are cooking apples'.* A first set of apparent characteristics is the system of degrees of stress placed on each syllable. But others can be imagined: e.g. all the correct grammatical transformations of the sentence form a set. In this case, one of the elements of $App(S)$ will be the proposition that ('are they cooking apples?') is a grammatically correct sentence.

Let us then assume that a first theory $T_1 = A_1 + Str_1(S)$ explains a system of apparent characteristics $App(S)$ pertaining to segment S, whereas a second theory $T_2 = A_2 + Str_2(S)$ explains a system $App_2(S)$. To clarify this point, the previous examples may be used again and S may be said to represent the segment 'they are cooking apples', $App_1(S)$—the stress on S, and $App_2(S)$—the set of grammatically correct transformations of S.

In this case, it is obviously better, from a scientific point of view, for $Str_1(S)$ to be merged with $Str_2(S)$. In other words, a single structural description will be preferred to descriptions varying with the system of explained characteristics. This can be expressed symbolically by writing that a general theory θ_1, such that:

$$A_1 + Str(S) \rightarrow App_1(S), A_2 + Str(S) \rightarrow App_2(S)\ldots,$$
$$A_n + Str(S) \rightarrow App_n(S).$$

will be prefixed to a general theory θ_2, such that:

$$A_1 + Str_1(S) \rightarrow App_1(S), A_2 + Str_2(S) \rightarrow App_2(S)\ldots,$$
$$A_n + Str_n(S) \rightarrow App_n(S).$$

In the case of theory θ_1, a single structural description obtains, whatever system of apparent characteristics one is trying to explain. In the case of theory θ_2, the descriptions are many and vary with the system of apparent characteristics whose analysis is attempted. To sum up, theory θ_1 can be considered more *comprehensive* than θ_2.

* This sentence can of course be understood in at least two different ways, and stressed accordingly.

These remarks are very important for analysing the psychological implications of the concept of *structural description*. In fact, while the structural description of a segment is meaningful only within theory $A + Str(S)$ and cannot by any means be viewed as *absolute*, the possibility remains that one structural description will be preferred to another, by reference to the criteria of *generality* and *comprehensiveness*, defined earlier. In the case of Chomsky and Miller's theory, there are reasons to believe that the structural description of segments as logical trees or systems of classified brackets is appropriate in so far as it is conducive to a fruitful theory.

As a limiting case, it is conceivable that one structural description could be proved better than any other. However, this test is postponed until the terminal phase of the research, and meanwhile any structural description necessarily retains the status of a scientific hypothesis, i.e. of a proposition temporarily held to be valid, but which new facts may invalidate. In brief, even if the most favourable conditions are posited and if one structural description is assumed to be better than all the others, the concept of structure still remains separated from the concept of essence by an unbridgeable gap.

Finally, let us consider an analysis such as that of stress on the message 'small boys' school'. The theory outlined above shows that a person wishing to convey the message 'small school for boys' behaves *as if* he applied the calculation defined by $A + Str(S)$. In other words, everything occurs as if the stress placed on the message resulted from a calculation defined by the theory $A + Str(S)$. However, if one were to identify with the individual who is receiving the message, and not with the one who is conveying it, only the apparent characteristics of the system are known to him, or, more accurately, *perceived* by him. In this case, he must, in order to understand the meaning of the message, solve the problem of deducing the structural characteristics from the apparent ones. If this comment is applied to the example discussed, the decoding of the message 'small boys' school' may be conceived as a calculation enabling one to deduce the structural description [$_B$ small ($_A$ boys' school) $_A$] $_B$ from the hierarchy of stresses.

Although this aspect of the analysis is not stated by Chomsky and Miller (at least in the texts referred to here), it is clear that a theory of stress must enable one to understand not only how a message is correctly *encoded* by the sender, but how it is correctly *decoded* by the receiver.

In other words, the problem is to know whether the 'structure' of a system may be unambiguously deduced from a knowledge of axioms A and of the apparent characteristics $App(S)$. In the examples quoted here, the process is reversed, since one can demonstrate from A that the stress 'small^3 boys'^{1} school' is incompatible with the structure $[_B$ small $(_A$ boys' school$)_A]_B$. These remarks will be summarized by stating that, in the context of the present example, the concept of structure is defined not only by formula (1), but also by the complementary formula:

$$(2) \qquad A + App(S) \xrightarrow{\text{Calculation}} Str(S).$$

Provisional definition of the concept of structure in the context of an operative definition

The hypothesis whose demonstration will be attempted in this chapter and in the next is that formulae (1) and (2) provide, in a way, the basic definition of the concept of structure in the context of effective definitions. The phrase 'in a way' is used intentionally, to convey that this basic definition is an ideal one which, as will be seen later, cannot always apply literally.

A corollary of this definition is that the structure of an object cannot be defined, in this type of context, by reference to concepts such as 'configuration of parts within a whole', 'a whole irreducible to the sum of its parts', 'system of relationships', etc. In short, the definition of the concept of structure cannot in this case be obtained by reference to its synonymic associations.

It can only be understood if a scientific language is used. As is shown by the formulae associated with its definition, this language includes the 'terms' S (system), A (axioms set), $App(S)$ (apparent characteristics of the system), *Calculation*, $Str(S)$ (structure of system S) and the relationships '+' and

'→'. The expression $x + y$ means that the whole set of propositions in x and in y is being considered, whereas the relationship $x → y$ means that y can be deduced from x.

Given this vocabulary, the concept of structure is defined by formulae (1) and (2). In other words, the structural analysis of a system may be defined as a theory which allows for the deduction of apparent characteristics (first formula). In reverse, it should be possible to deduce the structure from the theory and the apparent characteristics. As was mentioned at the start, the concept of structure is thus connected with a class of specific theories which could be named 'systems theories'.[7]

These hypotheses will be discussed at length later, but several comments should be made at this stage.

As has already been said, the definition of the concept of structure, summarized by the two formulae quoted above, is an ideal one. Hence there will be cases when formula (1) is discarded and the definition of the concept of structure reduces to formula (2). The following chapter will show that this is characteristic of Jakobson's structural phonology, as well as of Harris's and many other authors'.

It will also be seen that the set of axioms A, indispensable for the definition of the concept of structure in the context of effective definitions, may have characteristics which vary from one example to the other. Thus in the example given by Chomsky–Miller, axioms A are *general* in principle. In other words, formula (1) may be made more explicit in this case and may read: '$A + Str(S) \xrightarrow{\text{Calculation}} App(S)$, *for any S*'. The phrase 'for any S' is, of course, an ideal one: Chomsky–Miller's structural analysis has not been and cannot be proven to hold valid for all Ss. Yet its pretension to being general is implicit in its very logic. By contrast, in other cases, the axioms are strictly limited to applications to specific instances.

This is only one of many possible distinctions. Generally speaking, the theories associated with the concept of 'structural analysis' may, as all theories, be more or less convincing, more or less amenable to verification and proof. These differences can therefore induce the feeling that the word 'structure' does not have the same meaning in different contexts, although its definition may in all cases be reduced to our two formulae, made sufficiently explicit.

Moreover it is hardly surprising that in the context of effective definitions the concept of structure should conjure up the same synonymic *associations* and the same *oppositions* as it does in the context of intentional definitions. This point is not at all in contradiction with the fact that such associations and oppositions play no part in the case of an operative definition of the concept of structure. They are merely secondary consequences of this definition.

To consider, for example, the opposition 'structure–appearance', an examination of formulae (1) and (2) is enough to show that it derives naturally from the logic of structural analysis. Indeed structural analysis is, in a way, a theory of appearances, since the axiom and the structural description allow for a reconstruction of the phenomenal characteristics of the given system. Furthermore, the Chomsky–Miller example naturally conjures up the synonymous associations 'structure–coherence', 'structure–totality', 'structure–whole not reducible to the sum of its parts', 'structure–internal logic' etc. The confirmation of these associations in the given context springs from the fact that stress phenomena characteristic of a segment may all be deduced—at least in theory—from a general theory. Hence structural analysis finally demonstrates the *coherence* of facts that give or may give the impression of arbitrariness and contingency.

In addition, structural analysis implies that all the elements of *S* are taken into account and, in principle, that all the systems pertaining to one language are too. Consequently, a set of apparent characteristics can only be explained as a whole; this results also from formulae (1) and (2). By definition, a structural analysis covers the whole set of apparent characteristics of a system. Therefore it always grasps its object as a totality.

Hence it is now obvious that evoking the synonymic associations and oppositions of the word 'structure' is not specific to the particular example given here, but derives from the definition of the concept of structure contained in formulae (1) and (2).

Second example of type 1 : *analysis of kinship structures*

Our second example of a structure pertaining to type 1 is borrowed from the tradition of kinship-structures analysis. This example is of interest since it shows that a type 1 structure may either be associated with a mathematical model or not, depending on the cases considered. Thus, in the case of Chomsky and Miller's theory of stress in English, the deductive theory applied was non-mathematical. On the other hand, in the example which will now be considered, the concept of structure is associated with a mathematical model.

Incidentally it would be most interesting to systematically analyse the studies on kinship structures. Apart from the mathematical models of which an example will be given here, they, include analyses which, like those of Lévi-Strauss himself, rely on logical deduction rather than on model-building. Indeed it is certainly true that mathematical research stimulated by Lévi-Strauss's work and associated with the names of André Weil, Bush, Harrison White and others, covers only a small part of the facts outlined and analysed in the *Elementary Structures of Kinship*[8]—a limitation which does not detract from its interest.

The reader should bear these comments in mind when going through the broad outline given here of a well-known mathematical analysis carried out by Bush. He should remember that, while the concept of 'kinship structure' is always connected with a hypothetico-deductive theory of kinship systems, it has been possible to give to this theory the form of a mathematical model only in rather special cases.

Once more, the object of the analysis is well defined: it deals with the whole set of rules forbidding or allowing marriage as a result of kinship. Such rules are few in a given society. From a formal viewpoint, the object of the analysis is therefore of the same nature as in the previous example. It will be seen that the definition of the concept of structure arrived at by construction is also indistinguishable from that of the previous example, although the field to which it applies is of course quite different.

The psychological origin of research on kinship systems derives, as in the case of linguistic theory, from the mixed feeling of coherence and incoherence caused by the object investigated.

Thus, when examining marriage rules applying to first cousins in Kariera society, the researcher notes that it is forbidden to marry the daughter of one's father's brother, whereas it is allowed to marry either the daughter of one's father's sister or the daughter of one's mother's brother. These rules may be represented by using the habitual symbols, i.e. the sign '△' designates a male individual, the sign '○' a female and the sign '△ + ○' a conjugal couple. The fact that marriage between two individuals is allowed is recorded by the sign '(=)' and the fact that it is forbidden by '(≠)'. Marriage rules between first cousins in Kariera society are represented in figure 5.

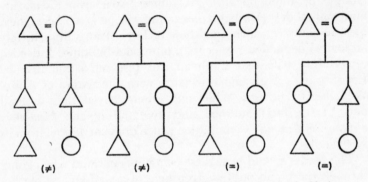

Figure 5: The Marriage Rules between First Cousins in Kariera Society

The feeling of arbitrariness[9] induced by these rules is confirmed if they are compared with those of another society, that of the Tarau. In the latter case, any marriage between cousins is prohibited, except marriage with the daughter of one's mother's brother. The marriage rules between first cousins in Tarau society are represented in figure 6.

Incidentally it should be noted in the connection that the sense of oddity induced by such facts is—as in the previous example—merely the counterpart of the inadequacy characterizing classical theories, be it classical grammar in the case of stress phenomena or pre-structuralist ethnography in that of marriage rules.

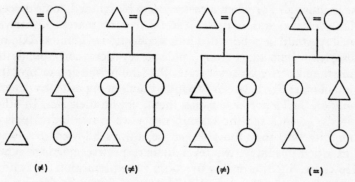

Figure 6: The Marriage Rules between First Cousins in Tarau Society

Here again, the system of marriage rules may be explained by reference to a set of axioms. These axioms, whose formulation is borrowed from Kemeny, Snell and Thompson, [24] are the following:

1. Each member of society S belongs to a marriage type.
2. Two individuals may marry if they belong to the same marriage type and only if they do.
3. The marriage type of an individual is determined only by his sex and by the marriage type of his parents.
4. Two boys and two girls whose parents belong to a different type are of different type themselves.
5. The permission or prohibition of marriage between two individuals of different sex depend only on the kinship tie between them.
6. No man can marry his sister.
7. It is always possible for some descendants of two individuals to intermarry.

These axioms have a dual origin. Axioms 1 to 5 are in fact the formal expression of ethnographic observations. In the societies examined, the rules permitting or prohibiting marriage are not formulated as a function of kinship ties, but through a classification of individuals, based in turn on the classification of their parents. Incest prohibition is then introduced by stating that classes are compatible or incompatible with each other from the viewpoint of marriage. Axiom 7 may be considered as functional. For when a caste system is excluded, some descendants of two individuals must be free to marry. Otherwise society would be subdivided into a collection of familes. Axiom 5 also, while reflecting ethnographic observations, corresponds to a functional prerequisite: it states that the permission or prohibition of marriage between two individuals of opposite sex depend only on the *kinship tie* between them, not on their *type*. In other words, given a specific kinship tie between two individuals of opposite sex, they must either be always allowed or always forbidden to marry, whatever their respective marriage types. However, since according to axiom 2 the permission or prohibition of marriage automatically results from the identity or difference of types, two individuals connected by a specific kinship tie must consequently either always belong to the same type—whatever it may be—or always belong to different types. In other words, it must be impossible to find situations in which, given the same kinship ties between them, *Ego* and *Alter* could, for example, either both belong to type t_1 or belong to types t_2 and t_3 respectively. Otherwise incest rules would become inextricably complicated, since the permission and the prohibition of marriage would depend not only on marriage types, but also on kinship ties. In fact, the classification into marriage types has an important function in pre-literate societies, since it expresses in simple terms a legislation which, if it were to be expressed by reference to kinship ties, would be extremely complex.

Let us accept this set of axioms and assume that the rules of type transmission are as outlined in Table II, which shows that four marriage types are defined in the society envisaged. When the parents are of type t_1, the son is of type t_3 and the daughter of type t_4; when the parents are of type t_2, the son is of type t_4 and the daughter of type t_3, etc.

It can be ascertained that these transmission rules tally with the axioms. Thus the reference made to the 'type *of the* parents' is in accordance with axiom 2, since two individuals can marry only if they belong to the same marriage type. Furthermore the table shows that the child's marriage type is in fact determined only by his sex and by the marriage type of his parents. It is therefore in accordance with axiom 3 and will also be seen to comply with axiom 4. Indeed the son's and the daughter's marriage types are permutations of the parents' marriage types. Consequently parents of different type beget children of different type. Axiom 6 is also compatible with the table; since the daughter's type is always different from the son's, a man always belongs to a type which is different from his sister's and hence, by virtue of axiom 2, cannot marry her. The table can also be shown to comply with axioms 5 and 7.

Table II. *Rules of type transmission in Kariera Society*

Type of parents	Type of son	Type of daughter
t_1	t_3	t_4
t_2	t_4	t_3
t_3	t_1	t_2
t_4	t_2	t_1

Thus let us examine the kinship tie symbolized by Figure 5a and assume that the couple of grandparents symbolized by the first line belong to type t_1. By virtue of Table II, their male children are of type t_3. But when an individual belongs to type t_3, his son is t_1 and his daughter t_2. Therefore, in this case, an individual cannot marry the daughter of his father's brother.

The same reasoning may be applied to the cases of grandparents belonging to types t_2, t_3, or t_4. In all cases, a man always belongs to a marriage type different from that of his father's brother's daughter. The analysis which readers could make in detail, if they wished, is summarized by figure 7.

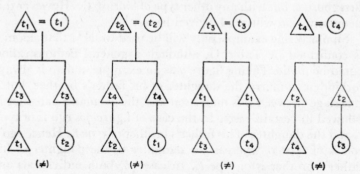

Figure 7 : Whatever the marriage type of his grandparents, no man may marry the daughter of his father's brother

Similarly the marriage type symbolized by figure $1b$ (a man's marriage to the daughter of his mother's sister) is always prohibited, whatever the marriage type of his grandparents. However a man is always allowed to marry either the daughter of his father's sister or the daughter of his mother's brother, regardless of the type to which his grandparents belonged.

Let us take for example the case of marriage to the daughter of one's father's sister. If grandparents belong to type t_1, the father is of type t_3 and the father's sister of type t_4. Hence ego is of type t_1 since his father belongs to type t_3. But the daughter of his father's sister is also of type t_1, since her mother is of type t_4. If grandparents belong to type t_2, it can similarly be shown that both ego and the daughter of his father's sister are of type t_2. Finally they both belong to type t_3 if their grandparents are of type t_3 and to type t_4 if their grandparents are of type t_4. Thus whatever type his grandparents belong to, a man is always allowed to marry the daughter of his mother's sister in a society characterized by the transmission rules shown on Table II and by the set of axioms described above.

These analyses show that Table II is compatible with axiom 5. Since two individuals of different sex who are related to each other in any way are always either of the same type or of different type, whatever type their grandparents belonged to, consequently the permission or prohibition of marriage between them depends in fact only upon their degree of kinship.

Axiom 5 could be demonstrated not only in connection with first cousins, but with any other type of kinship tie. However this demonstration will not be given here.

Similarly one example only will be used to show that axiom 7 is confirmed by Table II, although a general demonstration could be made. Taking figure 7 as an example, a man is always forbidden to marry the daughter of his father's brother, but a marriage between this man's son and this woman's daughter is allowed in certain cases. In the case of figure $7a$, ego is of type t_1 and the daughter of his father's brother of type t_2. Hence ego's son is of type t_3 whereas the daughter of the daughter of his father's brother is of type t_3. In case $7b$, both individuals are of type t_4. On the other hand, they belong to types t_1 and t_2 respectively in the cases of kinship ties symbolized by figures $7c$

and $7d$. Therefore this example shows that some descendants of the individuals represented on the first line of figure 7 may intermarry in accordance with axiom 7. Moreover it shows that ego's son is always authorized to marry the daughter of the daughter of his father's brother. In accordance with the requirements of axiom 5, this marriage depends therefore only on the nature of the kinship tie between the parties.

Although this fact has not been fully demonstrated, let us admit that Table II is in fact compatible with all axioms from 1 to 7.

What matters here is the recognition that the set of axioms and the transmission rules of Table II define a *calculation*, which results in the formulation of a system of rules allowing or prohibiting marriage that coincide exactly with the rules observed by ethnographers in Kariera society.

Although transmission rules have not been given any name designating their logical function, they clearly play a role which is identical with what we called in the previous example the 'structural description' of system S (in accordance with Chomsky and Miller's terminology), an expression abbreviated as $Str(S)$. As in the previous case, $Str(S)$ is a set of propositions which make sense only in relation to a set of axioms, and must be compatible with these axioms.

If the rules formulated in Table II are designated by $Str(S)$ and the set of axioms by A, formula (1) employed in the previous sub-section is again found to obtain. Again A and $Str(S)$ define a calculation which results in formulating the apparent characteristics of the system, i.e. in this case of the rules allowing or prohibiting marriage. Thus one can write once more:

$$A + Str(S) \xrightarrow{\text{Calculation}} App(S)$$

Let us now examine the other example mentioned at the beginning of this section, namely that of Tarau society.

If the set of axioms A is retained and if the rules summarized in Table III are defined as $Str(S)$, an analysis similar to the previous one may be conducted to show on the one hand that this table is compatible with A, on the other that the whole $A + Str(S)$ results in a calculation whose outcome coincides exactly

G

with the set of rules allowing or prohibiting marriage which is adopted in Tarau society. In particular the reader can check that the only type of marriage between first cousins to be authorized is between ego and the daughter of his mother's brother. Yet ego's marriage to either the daughter of his father's sister or the daughter of his mother's sister is prohibited.

The fact that A may apply to two different societies and allow for the definition of a calculation whereby the 'apparent characteristics' of these societies are deduced shows that this set of axioms possesses a certain degree of generality.

This impression of generality is confirmed by the knowledge that facts characterizing a much wider range of archaic societies are explained by this theory. In the societies studied by Lévi-Strauss and his disciples, ethnographic observation has shown that marriage rules deal differently with so-called 'cross' cousins. Marriage between parallel cousins is generally prohibited.

In fact the prohibition of marriage between parallel cousins happens to be a *general* consequence of the set of axioms A. In other words, whatever rules define $Str(S)$, if they are to be compatible with A, as they must be for the theory to be coherent, marriage between parallel cousins is prohibited. To put it differently, the prohibition of marriage between parallel cousins is not a consequence of the set of propositions $A + Str(S)$, but only of the propositions contained within A. This can be shown by reformulating the comments made about the axioms set A.

Firstly, whatever types of marriage occur in a society, the types of marriage permitted to a son, as well as to a daughter must be obtained by a *permutation* of the parents' marriage types. Moreover the son's type must always differ from the daughter's (otherwise axioms 2 and 6 would be incompatible). It results from these conditions that when two brothers or two sisters have children of the same sex, these children belong to different types. Hence marriage between parallel cousins is always prohibited, *whatever transmission rules obtain*. In other terms, if $Str(S)$ is compatible with A, marriage between parallel cousins is always prohibited, whatever $Str(S)$ may be.

This accounts for the apparent oddity due to the fact that marriage between parallel cousins is generally forbidden, whereas marriage between *ego* and the daughter of his father's sister is sometimes allowed, as in Kariera society, and sometimes forbidden, as in Tarau society.

A comment must be made at this stage: while it is easy to decide that a theory is false—by noting that at least one of its consequences contradicts observation—it is more difficult to analyse the psychological mechanism whereby conviction is attained. The difficulty is increased when—as is nearly always the case in the human sciences—the theory accounts for part of the facts known in a given field rather than for all of them. Indeed one can always wonder to what extent a *segmental* theory is a mere *ad hoc* representation incapable of truly explaining the fragment of reality to which it refers.

In the case of the analysis outlined here, it can be established that the set of axioms accompanied by appropriate 'structural descriptions' does correctly reproduce the marriage rules adopted by some societies. This is a remarkable result in itself. Furthermore one's trust in the explanatory power of the theory is increased when the general consequences of A are seen to correspond to facts which are very general in character since they pertain to groups of societies. In other words, *general* facts correspond to *general* propositions (deduced only from A) whereas the rules which vary from one society to the other are consequences of $A + Str(S)$. The degree of trust inspired by this theory is reinforced by this concordance between the level of logical generality possessed by its basic propositions and the empirical generality of the facts for which it accounts.

These comments are intended to illustrate the complexity of the logical and psychological mechanisms whereby a theory carries conviction. They also indicate that, while the concept of structure is always defined in the contexts discussed here with formulae (1) and (2) and is always associated with the notion of a systems theory, these theories may nevertheless vary considerably with regard to the manner in which evidence is produced. A comparison between the two examples given above would suffice to confirm this point. Although they are very closely related, their claims to validity do not rest on the same bases. Chomsky–Miller's theory of stress is more *general* than Bush's theory: it applies to a wider category of systems. On the other hand, Bush's model possesses certain logical attributes which confer upon it a much greater *credibility* than any *ad hoc* theory could have.

Hence a structural analysis may be more or less convincing. It does not follow however that the concept of 'structure' is homonymous.

Finally it should be noted that formula (2), i.e.

$$A + App(S) \xrightarrow{\text{Calculation}} Str(S)$$

applies to the examples analysed above. In other words, it is possible to deduce the transmission rules of types $Str(S)$ compatible with A from the set of axioms A and the apparent characteristics $App(S)$ of a system. In this case, $App(S)$ is the whole set of rules allowing or forbidding marriage which characterize system S.

It follows from this that the concept of structure has a single meaning in the two contexts studied above. In both cases, the object analysed has the characteristics of a *well-defined* system. In both, the theory takes the form of a testable hypothetico-deductive system. Moreover in both cases the definition of the concept of structure can be reduced to formulae (1) and (2).

The comments made in connection with the previous example are therefore equally pertinent to this one. The concept of structure is only defined in it with reference to the terminology summed up by formulae (1) and (2). The fact that the usual associations and oppositions of the concept of structure are evoked in this context can be explained in the same way. In so far as structural analysis is the theory of a system of facts, these facts must necessarily be explained as a totality and hence must reveal a coherence which contradicts the impression of arbitrariness produced by the apparent characteristics of the system.

It is so unavoidable for these synonymic associations to be conjured up that even the best philosophers are misled by them. Yet it is not pertinent to ask, as Ricoeur does for example [53], whether a structural analysis can convey the 'deep meaning' or the 'sense' of its object. If one is willing to overlook the philosophical nuances which separate the traditional concept of *essence* from the modern concepts of *sense* or *meaning*, this question is tantamount to asking whether the concept of structure as it appears in the context of 'structural analysis' can be identified with the synonymic association 'essence'.

One can answer that the concept of structure necessarily conjures up—in this context as in others—the synonymic association 'essence'. This is simply due to the fact that a structure is always the theory of a system of appearances. But the concept of structure is no more reducible to that of 'essence' than is the concept of *hypothesis* to that of *provisional affirmation*. 'Structure' as used here means 'testable theory of a system of apparent characteristics'. Therefore it 'reveals' its object just like any scientific theory.[10] To answer the question whether the essence of the object is thereby revealed requires an act of faith. Such an act may consist in holding the scientific theory representing the 'structure' of an object as the revelation of its 'essence'. This attitude corresponds to a *scientist's* outlook since science is expected to solve the philosophical issue of essences. Such an act of faith may alternatively consist in admitting that a form of knowledge exists which is sufficiently well-defined to be proclaimed superior to scientific knowledge. It is preferred here to adopt an intermediate position by admitting that the concepts of 'structure' and of 'essence' belong to two different languages—just like 'hypothesis' and 'provisional affirmation'.

To conclude this section, it should be pointed out that the two cases analysed—stress in English and the analysis of kinship structures—represent, so to speak, ideal cases, since theory construction is in both cases concerned with a set of systems that are naturally *defined* and whose description is easy. In other cases, as will be apparent in the following sections, the language defined by formulae (1) and (2) is applied to systems that are not naturally defined. Hence an arbitrary decision must be made at the start to transform the naturally undefined system into an artificially defined one. As for the concept of structure, it retains in these contexts pertaining to type 2 the same meaning as in the contexts of type 1, illustrated by the two previous examples. In other words it is strictly defined by formulae (1) and (2). The only difference is that this time 'structural analysis' deals with an *artificial* system.

Example of structure pertaining to type 2

The example selected to illustrate this type of structural analysis has been borrowed from sociology. It consists of a situation, very common in the analysis of sociological survey data, in which the individuals making up a population have been characterized by reference to a set of variables, and the problem arises of determining the 'structure' of the relationships between these variables.[11]

To clarify this point, a research project involving the analysis of a set of data on the voting intentions of a voters' sample during the American presidential election of 1940 will be used as an example. The data analysed was relatively simple: the same sample of voters had been polled several times during the electoral campaign. Two characteristics observed at two different stages will be considered here. The first concerned the political preference of the respondent (Democratic or Republican). The second concerned the respondent's attitude towards the Republican candidate (Wilkie).

This time the object analysed is an *artificial* one. In fact, there is no need to consider only these four characteristics (or more precisely these two characteristics observed twice over). It is easy to imagine other characteristics susceptible of accounting for voting behaviour. The number of observations could also be increased. Yet the 'structure' of this system can be analysed.

The results observed are reproduced in Table IV. It shows, for example, that only 6 out of 135 people who had favoured the Republican Party and its candidate modified their attitude on either point. By contrast, out of 35 people who had expressed simultaneously a liking for the Republicans and a dislike for the Republican candidate, 12—i.e. over a third—modified their attitude. The change had tended towards the voters harmonizing their attitudes towards the candidate with their political preferences. The same phenomenon can be observed if one considers the 24 people who during the first interview stated that they favoured the Democratic Party and the Republican candidate. By contrast, out of seventy-two people who had stated a preference for the Democratic Party and a dislike of the Republican candidate, only four changed their minds.

Table IV. *Voting preferences and attitudes towards the Republican candidate at two different interviews* (according to Lazarsfeld et al. [28])

First interview	Party candidate	Second interview				Total
		+ +	+ −	− +	− −	
Republicans favouring the Republican candidate (+ +)		129	3	1	2	135
Republicans against the Republican candidate (+ −)		11	23	0	1	35
Democrats favouring the Republican candidate (− +)		1	0	12	11	24
Democrats against the Republican candidate (− −)		1	1	2	68	72
TOTAL		142	27	15	82	266

These data are obviously clear and easy to interpret. Table IV, which is a set of interdependent elements, possesses a *'structure'* in the sense used in *intentional* contexts. In such a simple case, it is easy to construct a theory of the interdependence of these elements. The *structure* of this table—in the sense used in operative contexts—may therefore be obtained by intuitive analysis. However, one can easily conceive of situations in which three rather than two observed characteristics must be analysed on three rather than two occasions. If such were the case, assuming that the characteristics investigated were dichotomous (limited to two possibilities), the data would not be presented in a table comprising sixteen elements, but in eight tables of $8 \times 8 = 64$ elements. These figures increase rapidly with the number of characteristics and of observation periods. Therefore, even in comparatively simple cases, intuitive analysis becomes difficult. It would definitely become impossible if one wanted to analyse the relationships between four dichotomous characteristics observed on three occasions, since it would require the 'simultaneous'[12] analysis of 16 tables comprising 16×16 elements each.

It would therefore be of interest to devise a formal procedure whereby the *structure* of processes such as that described in Table IV could be defined, not only in cases when small numbers of characteristics are observed on two occasions, but in the general case of n characteristics observed on m occasions.

While the application of this procedure could not fail to confirm the results of intuitive analysis in the case of Table IV, it becomes indispensable when numbers n and m exceed 3 or even 2. Incidentally, this is an interesting example of a situation in which the need for a mathematical language occurs only when intuition becomes powerless to analyse a structure. This confirms the fact that the concept of structure is not necessarily connected with that of mathematical model, but only with the wider concept of *theory*.

When, as in Table IV, $n = m = 2$, the theory consists in propositions such as: in the process of attitude crystallization, the voter's preference for a candidate tends to harmonize with his basic political allegiance. Hence it is possible to directly deduce, without using any mathematical model, that 'unstable' attitudes $(-+)$ $(+-)$ will respectively give way to $(++)$ and $(--)$. In such a case, the consequences of a set of axioms can be directly deduced and their concordance with observed data can be checked. This can be expressed by the statement that the structure of Table IV is directly *legible*. However, in more complex cases it becomes impossible to determine intuitively whether a hypothesis is confirmed by observation or not. A formal model becomes necessary instead.

The example of Table IV will be retained for the sake of clarity in discussing the latter procedure, although its usefulness would only become apparent if more complex cases were quoted.

Table IV may be briefly interpreted as follows: the data seem to show that the two attitudes investigated are characterized by a degree of inertia. In other words, they tend to remain unchanged from one interview to the other. This is shown by the fact that out of 266 persons interviewed, 232 are located on the axis of Table IV. Moreover it seems possible to postulate a trend towards the two attributes being harmonized by an adjustment of the attitude towards a candidate to the preference for a political party. These attitudes $(+-)$ (Republicans disliking Republican candidate) and $(-+)$ (Democrats liking Republican candidate) can be viewed as unstable. It is assumed that attitude $(+-)$ must give way to attitude $(++)$ and attitude $(-+)$ to attitude $(--)$. Yet this change need not necessarily occur, as the trend towards harmonizing attitudes is offset by their inertia.

This hypothetical process may be illustrated by a diagram such as those which economists have been using ever since Tinbergen [56]. This diagram appears in figure 8.

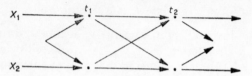

Figure 8: Flow diagram corresponding to the process of Table IV

The points located on the top line represent the characteristic 'political preference', which may be designated by x_1. Those located on the bottom line represent the variable 'attitude towards the Republican candidate', designated by x_2. The vertical alignment of the points indicates successive periods in time. On this diagram, two such periods, designated by symbols t_1 and t_2, are represented, corresponding with the two series of interviews. It is easy to interpret this diagram. The horizontal arrows of the upper line indicate the inertia of characteristic x_2, which could alternatively be expressed by the statement that attitudes towards the candidate tend to be stable over time. The transversal arrows indicate the delayed impact of each variable on the other. Thus the arrow drawn from point (x_1) to point (x_2) indicates that the political preferences expressed during the first interview tend to influence attitudes towards the Republican candidate at the time of the second interview.

On both sides of the points symbolizing the two interview times, a network of arrows similar to that which indicates the actions of the two variables x_1 and x_2 between t_1 and t_2 has been drawn. It is intended to convey the hypothesis that the process observed at two times t_1 and t_2 remains unchanged over a longer period. It is thus assumed that if a third interview had been taken at a time t_3, a process with a 'structure' similar to that of the previous period would have been observed.

An arrow such as that which connects points (x_1, t_1) and (x_2, t_2) indicates therefore that the condition of variable x_1 at time t_1 determines with a degree of probability that of the same variable at time t_2. Assuming that this influence can be measured[13] and that this measure is designated by $a_{11 \cdot 12}$ (action of variable x_1 at time t_1 upon variable x_1 at time t_2), the hypothesis expressed by the arrow may be stated as follows:

The probability of being in condition x_1 at time t_2 when one is in condition x_2 at time t_1 is a function of $a_{11 \cdot 12}$.

Similarly, if the effect of variable x_2 at time t_1 on variable x_1 at time t_2 is designated by $a_{21 \cdot 12}$, the probability of being in condition x_1 at time t_2, knowing that at t_1 one was in condition x_1 and x_2, may be expressed as a function of $a_{11 \cdot 12}$, and $a_{21 \cdot 12}$.

There is no need to go into the details of this model. It is enough to understand that a system of equations may be associated with the hypotheses which have first been expressed in words and later represented by arrows. This system is a model whose parameters are the measures of influences $a_{11 \cdot 12}$, $a_{21 \cdot 12}$, etc., each of which corresponds to an arrow on figure 5. The parameters associated with these arrows are indicated on figure 9. Additional hypotheses may naturally be introduced if necessary: for example, it will be posited that the functions are *linear*. The value of all parameters will then be obtained by solving the system of equations.

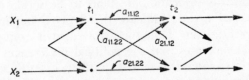

Figure 9: Parameters associated with the flow diagram of figure 8

According to a practice introduced by econometricians, these parameters will be said to define the *structure* of the process which occurred in the interval between the two observations, or they will be called the 'structural' parameters of the model.

It is immediately noticeable that the 'structure' of the process is defined only in relation to the equations that express conditional probabilities as functions of parameters. It is always possible to write other equations, depending on the hypotheses one wishes to introduce. Different hypotheses obviously result in different equations and, consequently, in different evaluations of the parameters or even in the introduction of new parameters. Hence the 'structure' of the process is described in terms which vary with the hypotheses adopted. However, this does not lead to an inconclusive relativism, as it is generally possible to choose between two theories by confronting the data yielded by observation with an estimate of these data based on the estimated structural parameters. If the hypotheses incorporated in the equations are sound, the estimate should produce acceptable results.[14]

To illustrate this point, the estimated results arrived at in the case used as an example here are reproduced in Table V. The theory used in this connection is that which was summed up by the flow diagram in figure 8. It has been assumed that the effects indicated by arrows in this figure were cumulative.

Table V. *Estimate of the data of Table IV on the basis of structural parameters*

First interview	Party candidate	Second interview				Total
		+ +	+ −	− +	− −	
Republicans favouring the Republican candidate (+ +)		126	5	3	1	135
Republicans against the Republican candidate (+ −)		13	22	0	0	35
Democrats favouring the Republican candidate (− +)		0	0	15	9	24
Democrats against the Republican candidate (− −)		0	2	3	67	72
TOTAL		139	29	21	77	266

Table V shows the date estimated on the basis of this model to be close to the observed data. The theory by reference to which the parameters were estimated may therefore be held valid. It should be noted that the values attributed to the structural parameters are in accordance with the hypotheses that can be formulated when the *structure* of Table IV is intuitively analysed. The values of these parameters are as follows:

$$a_{11 \cdot 12} = 0 \cdot 956$$
$$a_{21 \cdot 22} = 0 \cdot 583$$
$$a_{11 \cdot 22} = 0 \cdot 342$$
$$a_{21 \cdot 12} = 0 \cdot 018$$

If one refers to figure 8, which sums up the meaning of these parameters, one sees that these results express the following facts. Firstly, the two characteristics appear to display a certain inertia, since $a_{11 \cdot 12}$ and $a_{21 \cdot 22}$ are significantly different from nought. But the inertia of the former exceeds that of the latter: it is as if political attitude towards the party induced change in the second attitude. This is confirmed by the fact that as the respective values of $a_{11 \cdot 22}$ and $a_{21 \cdot 12}$ show, variable x_1 has an important deferred effect on x_2, whereas x_2 has practically no effect on x_1.

This is now sufficiently clear for us to investigate the meaning of the concept of structure in the present context.

Firstly, this example, although it is specific, belongs to a very large family of examples pertaining to the same type. Thus all econometric models are of this type. They always consist in expressing certain observed quantities as a function of other observed quantities and of 'structural' parameters. The model is then solved by reference to these parameters and the validity of the 'structures' obtained is checked by investigating whether the estimated data fits in with the results of observation.

Having said this, it is easy to realize that the concept of structure in the context of the present example has exactly the same meaning as in previous examples. The equations of the model represent axioms which, when applied to the data or —to use the terminology introduced earlier—to the apparent characteristics of the system, define a calculation. The value of the structural parameters can then be deduced from this calculation. 'Formula (2)' can again be applied in this case and reads:

$$A + App(S) \xrightarrow{\text{Calculation}} Str(S).$$

Moreover the validity of the proposed theory will be tested by checking that the set of axioms supplemented by the estimated values of the structural parameters permits an accurate assessment of the data yielded by observation. As in previous cases, formula (1) therefore supplements formula (2). However, in this case formula (1), i.e.,

$$A + Str(S) \xrightarrow{\text{Calculation}} (App)S$$

assumes a specific function, since it describes the testing procedure which shows that a 'structural analysis' does provide an acceptable picture of reality.

Incidentally, the sociological model used as an example has an important advantage over the thousand-and-one econometric models which could have been selected in its place. Indeed it shows how a mathematical model is merely substituted for *intuition* when the analysed situation becomes too complex. In a case in which two characteristics only are observed on two occasions, the *structure* of a process such as that of Table IV is directly *legible*, since the interpretation of data can be checked by looking as the table. In a more complex case, the structure becomes *illegible*. The model then plays the part of a detecting instrument which makes this information *legible*. The legible information thus provided is nothing else than the set of *structural* parameters.

It should also be noted that defining the concept of structure by reference to our two basic formulae enables one to clarify the issue of the opposition between 'structure' and 'process'.

The example used here shows that one can refer—in an unambiguous way—to the 'structure' of a process. All that is required is for the system studied to have been observed on several occasions and analysed in the language defined by the two basic formulae. In this example, the data collected did not allow for the analysis of more than two consecutive observations. With these observations has been associated a structure, which appears in figure 10.

The only difference between this figure and the schema in figure 8 is that the values of the 'structural parameters' have now been entered above the corresponding arrows.

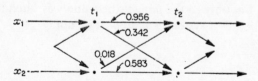

Figure 10: Structure of the process whose observation is recorded in Table IV

However, it is possible to imagine that the number of observations exceeds two. Let us assume, for example, that the
previous analysis is applied to a series of five observations made
at regular intervals. If the results obtained are similar to those
of figure 11, the process observed can be called 'structurally
stable', since the structural parameters are constant at all the
times considered.

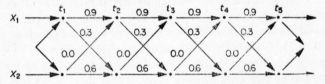

Figure 11 : Example of a process characterized by structural stability

On the other hand, different results could have been observed:
for instance, that the influence of political preference for a party
on the attitude towards the candidate steadily decreased, as in
the case of figure 12. In such a case, it would be possible to
detect structural change and to describe it unambiguously.

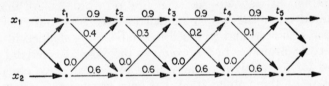

Figure 12 : Example of a process characterized by structural change

Therefore the concept of structure can easily be extended to
the analysis of processes. This is a simple consequence of the
definition given of this concept. If it is true that the concept of
structure is not connected to the content of the systems
analysed, but only to the *form* of their analysis, then it does not
matter whether a system is temporal or not.

Conclusion

This chapter may now be concluded by stating that the concept
of structure corresponds in all the cases examined to a single

definition, described by formulae (1) and (2). Formula (1)
shows that this concept is inseparable from a theory which has
the property of yielding consequences reproducing the apparent
characteristics of the system described. In other words, the
apparent characteristics and the theorems deduced from the
theory are one and the same. This is tantamount to saying
that the theory is designed to account for the whole set of
apparent characteristics of the system *as a totality*. Therefore it
naturally evokes the synonymic associations of the term 'structure', although in this case the meaning of the concept of
structure cannot be reduced to its associations. Formula (1)
symbolizes the stage of synthesis, which tests the compatibility
of the theory with observation. Formula (2), on the other hand,
represents the stage of analysis: it sums up the process whereby
the researcher, confronted with an object whose elements he
considers as interdependent, formulates hypotheses that are
intended to account for this interdependence. Although the
logical constructs associated with these various examples differ
from each other, they are always expressed in a language which
is summed up by the two basic formulae. Formula (2) expresses
the procedure by which the 'structure' of a system is obtained.
Formula (1) describes the 'testing' procedure by which one
ascertains that a *theory* is really acceptable, the concept of theory
being defined by the proposition contained in $A + Str(S)$.

Yet the concept of structure induces a feeling of homonymy
when examples of type 1 (analysis of stress in the English language, analysis of kinship structures) are compared with
examples of type 2 (factorial analysis, analysis of the process of
voting choice). The very fact that one talks of 'structural
anthropology' or 'structural linguistics', but not of 'structural
sociology' or 'structural economics', may be construed as an
indirect confirmation of this homonymy.[15] It is doubtful
whether such a difference in linguistic usage could be explained
by historical accidents. True, the switch to structuralism was
comparatively sharp in linguistics and in anthropology. But
economics resorted to 'structuralist' methods at an even earlier
date. In fact, the scientific approach characteristic of Chomsky's
structural syntax and of the structural analysis of kinship
cannot be distinguished from that which is applied in economics.

In all cases, the researcher starts from a set of data which he considers to be interdependent, formulates certain explanatory hypotheses, and ascertains that from these hypotheses the 'apparent characteristics' of the system he is trying to explain can actually be deduced. The same procedure could be found in many research projects pertaining to the sphere of sociology, as is shown by the example borrowed earlier from the sociology of voting behaviour. Nevertheless there are references to 'structural syntax' and to 'structural anthropology', not to 'structural sociology'. Since it is impossible to detect any fundamental difference between the 'structural methods' of these various disciplines, the origin of the distinction made between them must be found elsewhere. In our view, it consists in a difference between the *objects* of these disciplines rather than between their *methods*. In analysing the marriage rules obtaining in a society, one deals with a small number of facts which can easily be observed and described. In analysing a segment of the English language, one also deals with a limited set of facts whose observation is easy. By contrast, in an analysis of an economic system or even—on a more modest scale—of a voting preference, it is necessary to arbitrarily select a number of factors pertaining to the economic system, or a system of factors that determine the voter's decision. Nothing could prevent marriage rules from being a well-defined system, whereas the factors of this decision constitute an undefined system. *In a sense*, the concept of 'structure' does not therefore have the same *meaning* when one refers to the 'structures of kinship' and to the 'structure of the decision'. The feeling of homonymy is so strong that honest witnesses, unsophisticated about the history of science, believe structuralism to be the prerogative of anthropology and linguistics and suggest introducing it in other fields, as if the method—unlike the term—had not existed for a long while in such disciplines as sociology or economics. Yet this attitude is understandable: results are less spectacular when the object which is the starting point of the research is arbitrarily subdivided and reconstituted. It seems unsurprising that a mathematical order should prevail in such a case. On the other hand, when such an order exists in natural objects which are in no way the product of the observer's design—as in the case of marriage rules—it stimulates surprise, a sense of revelation: consequently, the structure is not located with the observer, but in the things observed, and one begins to wonder whether 'structuralism' is the means of discovering the 'essence' of the object.

As has already been said, it is unreasonable to ask whether the analysis of structures is an analysis of essence, as it would be absurd to wonder whether physics reveals the 'essence' of matter. A structure is either a scientific hypothesis or it is nothing. Now a scientific hypothesis can *hic et nunc* be the best possible, it can account for more facts that any other and comply with other criteria too. Yet it is essential that it should be possible to discard this hypothesis tomorrow in order to adopt a better one instead. To believe with some that 'structuralism' may reveal the hidden aspect of things or even to *wonder* whether structures describe the essence or the deep meaning of things prevents one from understanding the concept of structure. The questions thus asked are simply meaningless. But it is easy to understand that they should have been raised, since they are merely the reflection and the expression of the understandable surprise experienced when—as in the analysis of kinship structures—a mathematical order is discovered in a 'natural' object. This surprise is all the greater since to the superficial observer the object investigated seems to be an *aggregate* of unconnected elements.

However, this attitude only expresses the fact that a theory may be more or less surprising, more or less convincing. Indeed it is not enough that a theory be corroborated, or at least not falsified, for it to prove equally convincing to all. Its very nature stimulates complex psychological reactions and results in varying degrees of conviction.

In spite of these intrinsic characteristics of the theories associated with the concept of structure, this concept still has a well-defined meaning in all the contexts examined. The feeling of homonymy originates from specific contexts and is due in particular to some object-systems being well-defined, while others are *undefined*. This corresponds to a fact and must therefore be accepted.

Incidentally, what might be called 'magic structuralism'

H

originates from ignorance of these obvious facts—i.e., that the structural analysis of a system is the product of a theory and that the construction of effective theories depends upon the nature of the object and the conceptual tools available. As structuralism has yielded undoubtedly spectacular results in such disciplines as anthropology and linguistics, some have come to believe that these revolutions were due only to a change of approach in the metaphysical sphere. In their view, linguists transformed their discipline as soon as they realized that the elements of languages were organized in systems, in wholes of interdependent parts, in 'totalities distinct from the sum of their parts', etc. Such a statement is so oversimplified that it is both true and false. In fact, structuralist revolutions are initiated not when it is understood that languages, personalities, markets and societies are systems, but when the conceptual tools are devised that permit the analysis of these systems as systems. Yet some have believed that it was enough to consider an object as a system to achieve scientific change *ipso facto*. It is this belief that is called here 'magic structuralism'. As a result, in magic structuralism, structures are in effect assimilated to metaphysical essences. No method is required to attain them, only a certain mental or spiritual training is needed. The existence of such a magic structuralism is an additional source of confusion. It is merely mentioned here, as its analysis would go beyond the problem investigated in this book. The difference between structuralism as exemplified by Chomsky or by *The Elementary Structures of Kinship*, on the one hand, and what has been called magic structuralism on the other, can be compared to that which separates modern 'atomistic' physics from Democrites' theory.

4

The Concept of Structure in the Context of Operative Definitions: Structures without Apparent Axioms

In the previous chapter examples of structures associated with apparent axioms have been considered. In all those cases, it was possible to show that the structure of the given system was always defined in relation to a set of axioms. The hypothesis whose corroboration will be attempted now is that such a 'structure of the concept of structure' exists also in the cases in which this concept, although in the context of an operative definition, does not appear to be associated with a set of axioms.

Examples of type 3

No study dealing with the concept of structure in the human sciences can dispense with a mention of structural phonology, a discipline which undeniably originated the great fashion surrounding the term *structure* in these sciences. Furthermore, the methods used in structural phonology are often regarded as the prototype of structuralist methods in the human sciences.

Therefore the meaning of the concept of structure in this type of context must be made clear.

Obviously the purpose is not to give a general outline, even a summary one, of structural phonology, but—in accordance with the method employed in previous chapters—to analyse closely a particularly significant example. This method offers some disadvantages: although structuralism is a badge worn by nearly all phonologists, although the general principles mentioned in the first chapter of this book are widely accepted, the application of these principles varies considerably from author to author—as Martinet [37] has demonstrated. Yet, in phonology as in other fields, the concept of structure possesses a single and perfectly clear meaning, in spite of the diversity of its applications. The definition given to it is simply a variation of that provided in the previous chapter.

A single example will show this to be the case: it will be taken from Harris's phonological analysis.

The aims and difficulties of structural phonology must be recalled briefly in order to put Harris's phonology in the proper context [21].

The purpose is to describe the sounds that convey 'spoken' messages by considering them as a system. Unlike classical phonetics, structural phonetics does not attempt to catalogue and describe the elements of those utterances as accurately as possible. This has been shown in Chapter 1 to be an impossible task. The problem consists rather in constructing the theory of the sounds conveying spoken messages. Its importance for linguistics is obvious and one cannot wonder that it should have been the first issue tackled by structural analysis. The basic problem of language is to know how a message may be coded as a flow of sounds and, in reverse, how this flow can be decoded to result in a meaningful message in the recipient's mind. In brief, the coding and decoding of a message always reduces to the recognition that a relationship which is unambiguous at two levels obtains between the message conveyed and a set of sounds. Hence language should be considered as a code and its properties studied as forming a code. This is tantamount to saying that the sounds which make up the segments of a language should be conceived as a system.

Consequently, one of the first tasks of phonology is to describe the elementary signs of this code, generally called phonemes. Yet two difficulties arise at the very outset. The first is the considerable variability observed in the production of sounds. The second is due to the fact that some variations in sound production are related to context, and serve no function in the coding and decoding of messages. The example of the initial sound in the French words *kilo* and *courage* is again a case in point: the sounds respectively transcribed as letter *k* and letter *c* are objectively very different from each other. However, this distinction is never utilized in the French language to *point to* a difference in meaning. It is a mere product of its environment: before *il* the phoneme *k* is pronounced as in *kilo*, while before *ou* the same phoneme *k* is pronounced as in *courage*.

These considerations show that the elementary sound entities of a language should be considered as classes of sounds rather than as sounds, strictly speaking. Thus the two sounds that begin the words *kilo* and *courage*, although objectively distinct, should be viewed as one entity. This abstract way of defining 'phonemes' is not devoid of difficulties. Firstly, one may wonder whether it is possible to arrive at a process which would permit an exhaustive cataloguing and classification of the elementary sounds of a language into 'phonemes'. Secondly, if phonemes are not sounds, but classes of sounds, it seems logical not to describe them any longer by reference to their attributes. In fact, the equivalent sounds pertaining to a class which defines a phoneme are objectively very different from each other. The solution proposed is not very convincing when the final aim is to explain the phenomenon of language rather than merely to devise a classification satisfactory to the mind: in order to decode the flow of sounds into a message, the sequence of elementary sounds must be identified by their acoustic properties. Linguists are acutely aware of the contradiction between the fact that phonemes should be considered as classes of sounds rather than as sounds and the necessity to describe the sounds associated with phonemes—a need which derives from the impossibility of two signals conveying a distinct information unless they are physically distinct themselves. According to André Martinet ([38], p. 67), 'probably the most delicate phonologic operation is this use of the phonic material, which is necessary to identify pertinent characteristics'. This contradiction has been so keenly felt that some authors do not even attempt to define phenomes by reference to their attributes or 'distinctive traits', but define them by the environment in which they are found. The first type of definition is 'paradigmatic', the second is 'syntagmatic'.

As has just been stated, the former approach results in an ambiguous definition of the object, since the purpose is to draw up a list of the objective characteristics of phonemes, which are themselves defined as classes of sounds. Hence a paradigmatic definition must be based on a compromise, which is unlikely to be unanimous. It is thus understandable that some authors, such as Harris, should have attempted to carry syntagmatic research as far as possible and deliberately neglected the sounds associated with phonemes. The advantage of such an approach is that it greatly diminishes the element of arbitrariness involved in describing the sound material of language. It will be seen that the solution arrived at by Harris represents a true 'classificatory model'. The method he outlines consists in positing a number of general classificatory principles, naturally selected in the light of theoretical concerns, and to *deduce* from them the structural description of the language investigated. In short, here as in the previous examples, the 'structure' of the object considered is the description derived from a deductive theory.

Let us first outline the operations by which Harris suggests that the phonological structure of a language should be analysed.

The first stage consists in determining the elementary segments of a language. A first difficulty immediately arises, namely how to decide whether a sound is 'elementary' or not. In order to solve it, Harris proposes a simple procedure which consists in carrying out first an intuitive and arbitrary segmentation. Thus—according to the example given by Harris—the expression 'I'll tack it' could be divided into four hypothetical elements: A ($= al$), T ($= t^h ae$), k, I ($= it$). Possible errors will then be corrected by a substitution test. To this end the broken-up segment will be compared with others: suppose the expression 'I'll pack it', has been split up as AP ($= p^h ae$) kI, the expression 'I'll tip it' as AQ ($= t^h i$) pI, and 'I'll dig it' as AD ($= di$) gI. One would then observe easily that the first part of T was substitutable for the first part of Q, the last part of T for the last part of P, etc. Gradually, the elementary segments t^h, ae and i would thus be isolated. The part of P not substitutable for a part of T would ultimately be identified as p^h. Similarly d would be identified as the part of D not substitutable for a part of Q. If these operations are carried out on a sufficiently large sample of utterances, they automatically result in a table of unique sound segments. In other words, this table will be independent from both the expressions initially chosen and their original segmentation.

After these preliminary operations, the problem consists in determining the phonologic structure of the given language from a syntagmatic, and not from a paradigmatic, definition of phonemes. This will be done by relying on the 'principle of pertinence', on which all phonologists agree and whereby two segments represent different phonemes only if they perform a distinct function. This gives a general form to the proposition that sounds, or—as they will henceforth be called—two elementary segments cannot be considered as structurally distinct if the apparent differences between them are not due to their environment.

The *calculation* proposed by Harris in order to arrive at this structural description is the following: firstly, having determined the elementary segments, all the contents in which they appear are recorded. This would obviously be an infinite task if no upper limit was given to the length of contexts. Yet to fix such a limit is to invite arbitrariness. However, this difficulty can easily be overcome since beyond a certain length there is no limitation on the possible elements of a context. Thus, if it is observed that a segment appears in contexts (CsC') and that (CsC') may occur in any context, all contexts ($———CsC'———$) will be ranked as equivalent within one class designated by $(C–C')$. For example, the context 'silence–vowel' in which the initial segment t^h of 'tack' occurs may itself be found in any context.

Consequently, a *finite* number of contexts may be defined in a language. The finite character of this number results from the concept of context being defined as a class of equivalent segments. From the phonological viewpoint, a language can therefore be characterized by a chart in which the segments are listed on one axis and the contexts along the other. The box that corresponds to the ith line and the jth column of the chart will remain blank if the jth segment is never found in the ith environment. Otherwise it will be marked with a cross.

Complementary segments are then those which never occur in the same context. Two complementary segments correspond therefore to two lines of the phonological chart, neither of which ever has a cross in the same column as the other. A pair of complementary segments is a pair of segments which cannot be held structurally distinct: since they never occur in the same context, they can never perform a distinguishing function in relation to each other.

If the relationship of complementarity which has thus been defined were *transitive*, there would be no difficulty in unambiguously defining the concept of 'phoneme' and in determining the 'phonemes' of a language by a quasi-mechanical procedure. A phoneme would be a class of equivalent segments defined by reference to this complementarity. Let us assume three segments s_i, s_j and s_k. If the relationships:

$$s_i \text{ complementary to } s_j$$

and

$$s_j \text{ complementary to } s_k$$

necessarily involved the accuracy of the relationship:

$$s_i \text{ complementary to } s_k,$$

a phoneme could be defined as a set of complementary segments. The structural description of a language would then be obtained by deduction from the definition of the phoneme as a sound element endowed with a distinguishing function.

However, the relationship of complementarity is not transitive. Additional rules must therefore be introduced to solve this problem of classification of elementary segments. Let us therefore assume a situation in which segment s_i is complementary to segment s_j and s_j to s_k, but s_i is not complementary to s_k. If the phoneme were merely defined as a class of complementary segments, s_i and s_k would have to be assigned to the same phoneme and so would s_j and s_k, but s_i and s_k to different phonemes, hence a contradiction.

An important comment should be made before outlining the additional rules suggested by Harris in order to resolve this difficulty. Resorting to a relationship of complementarity in order to distinguish between phonemes is a direct consequence of the structuralist view that the sound material of a language is made up of a stock of elementary signals. Yet this relationship cannot lead to an unambiguous classification of elementary segments. The additional rules introduced at this stage only serve to eliminate ambiguity. They are not directly derived from the theory of the phoneme as a signal and may be considered as matters of convention. On the other hand, it is obvious that whenever conventional rules are introduced within a set of axioms, the structural description of the object derived from these axioms becomes itself a product not only of the object's intrinsic properties, but also of these conventional rules. Therefore it cannot be considered as *unique*. Yet the introduction of conventional rules in a case such as the one examined here is clearly a consequence of the context in which it occurs. More precisely, it is produced by a contradiction between an end and a means. The phonologist's *aim* is to assign segments to phonemes (classes of segments that are distinct both in appearance and in structure). The *means* at his disposal consists in defining the concept of structural distinctiveness by references to a distinguishing function. All linguists are roughly agreed both on the aim and the means, since one of the main insights of structural phonology consists precisely in the statement that apparently distinct sounds may perform no distinguishing function. The contradiction consists in the fact that the relationship 'to belong to the same class' is transitive, whereas the 'complementarity' relationship is not. Another way of expressing this contradiction consists in saying that the classificatory rules derived from a consideration of the complementarity relationship do not allow for any satisfactory deduction. Finally, it must be realized that the introduction of conventional rules into the set of axioms is a consequence of the logical context.

These conventional rules will now be briefly examined.

First, it should be stressed that the very definition of the complementary relationship introduces an iterative process. As soon as two segments whose complementarity has been recognized are assigned to one phoneme, some contexts cease to be distinct. Consequently certain segments that appear complementary are no longer so, and must be assigned to distinct phonemes. Thus, when it is realized that in English segment t^h—which corresponds to the sound T followed by a slight aspiration—always occurs before a vowel and after a silence, whereas sound t unaspirated only occurs after a consonant (as in 'stone'), t and t^h must be assigned to one phoneme. All the contexts differing only in the distinction between t and t^h must from then on be viewed as identical.

This iterative process does not make the introduction of conventional rules unnecessary. It does not turn the relationship of 'complementarity to' into a transitive one.

The first rule introduced by Harris derives from the wish to define phonemes as entities independent from the environment in which they are found. To this end an attempt is made to assign segments to phonemes, so that each phoneme occurs in so far as possible in all environments through one or the other of its segments. If by 'freedom of occurrence' is meant the number of environments in which a phoneme occurs, the problem consists in maximizing the freedom of each phoneme. Thus it is observed that the unaspirated t that appears, for example, in 'stone' is complementary to t^h, as it appears, for example, in 'tack'; similarly, the p in 'spend' is complementary to t^h. It then becomes possible and reasonable to assign all the segments t and t^h, or all the segments p and t^h, to one phoneme. The rule of maximum freedom of occurrence operates here. Thus a phoneme to which segment t was assigned, but segment t^h was not, could not for example appear in the context 'silence–vowel' characteristic of the word 'tack'.

This first rule is supplemented by a second one whereby segments should be classified so as to make the context of phonemes as homogeneous as possible. Let us take, for example, the case of elementary segment a appearing in contexts C_1, segment b in contexts C_2 and C_3, segment c in contexts C_1 and C_2, and segment d in contexts C_3. It would be possible to assign to the same phoneme either a and b or a and d. By virtue of the second rule, the former decision will be made, since when one assigns a and b to the same phoneme it is possible to assign c and d to another, as c and d are complementary. Two phonemes whose environments are the same are thus obtained.

The third rule, which reflects a concern for economy, consists in reducing the number of phonemes to a minimum. Thus the choice made in the previous example would again be justified by reference to this rule. Indeed, if segments a and d, which are complementary, were assigned to the same phoneme, the four segments *a*, *b*, *c* and *d* would have to be assigned to three phenomes. Because *b* and *c* are not complementary, they could not be assigned to one phoneme; because they share common contexts with (a, d), they could not belong to the (a, d) phoneme. On the other hand, the four segments can be assigned to two phonemes by grouping together *a* and *b*, and then *c* and *d*.

Other rules analogous in character to those already analysed, but covering points of detail, will not be dealt with.

This set of rules exhausts the formal classificatory criteria that can be drawn up. Yet, as readers can easily ascertain, it does not allow for a satisfactory classification of elementary segments. Let us take, for example, the following four segments: *p* not followed by aspiration as in 'spoil', p^h followed by aspiration as in 'party', *t* not followed by aspiration as in 'stone', and t^h followed by aspiration as in 'tack'. The following complementarity relationships exist between them:

> *p* complementary to p^h,
> *p* complementary to t^h,
> *p* not complementary to *t*,
> p^h not complementary to t^h,
> p^h complementary to *t*,
> t^h complementary to *t*.

Thus one could either choose to assign *p* and p^h, on the one hand, and *t* and t^h, on the other, to the same phonemes, or alternatively, *p* and t^h, on the one hand, and *t* and p^h on the other. At a glance, the first classification seems more natural than the second. However, none of the formal rules—the most important of which have been outlined above—enables one to choose between the two solutions. Either decision would result in two phonemes whose environments would comply with the criteria of economy, maximum freedom of occurrence, and environmental homogeneity.

It is therefore necessary to introduce a new set of rules, taking into account the sound material which one had attempted to eliminate. Indeed, if the classification which groups *p* and p^h together appears more natural than the regrouping of *p* and t^h, it is ultimately for the sole reason that *p* and p^h are closer to each other from the viewpoint of articulation. The difference between p and p^h is the same as that between t and t^h: the two segments of each of these two groups are similar but for one aspiration. In the end Harris is thus compelled to reintroduce a search for 'correlations'. In order to assign a and b, on the one hand, and c and d on the other, to phonemes, the following conditions must be met:

(1) a and b must both appear in a class of environments C_1;

(2) c and d must both appear in a class of environments C_2;

(3) there must be no environment common to C_1 and C_2;

(4) there must exist a criterion by reference to which a is to c what b is to d (a condition which is sometimes expressed as follows: '$a:c::b:d$').

These conditions are fulfilled when $a = p$, $b = t$, $c = p^h$ and $d = t^h$. Indeed p and t are found in the same set of contexts (C_1), as are p^h and t^h (in contexts C_2). Furthermore, the contexts of p and t are distinct from those of p^h and t^h. Finally, p is to p^h what t is to t^h, since p^h and t^h are respectively distinguished from p and t by a phenomenon of aspiration. Consequently p and p^h will be assigned to one phoneme, and t and t^h to another.

What is the meaning of the concept of structure in this type of context?

Obviously Harris aims at defining a *calculation* whereby he could obtain the phonological structure of a language in a purely deductive and mechanical way, without any subjectivism. This calculation in turn embodies a series of theoretical propositions which are widely accepted by phonologists. They state that the sound material of a language is a set of signals, that these signals, in order to perform their function, should not be the product of their environment; that they must consequently be free to occur in any environment, etc. Yet it is difficult to couch this theory in completely formal terms. This is due, on the one hand, to the impossibility of arriving at a single decision in every case by applying the set of formal rules.

This has been shown by the example of the four segments p, p^h, t and t^h. It then becomes necessary to consider the 'sound material'. On the other hand, it is impossible to assert that the formal rules will not result in some cases in contradictory decisions: a classification may comply with the rule of maximum freedom of occurrence while infringing upon another rule.

In conclusion, the definition of the concept of structure in this context may be represented by formula (2) of the previous chapter

$$A + App(S) \xrightarrow{\text{Calculation}} Str(S)$$

The 'phonological structure' is obtained by applying a set of axioms to a system of apparent characteristics. These axioms may not be exactly as defined in the previous chapter, since the 'sound material' of messages must be taken into account. Likewise it may not be exactly a calculation, since the concept of *correlation* cannot be expressed in a fully formalized way: the relationship $a:c::b:d$ implies that a property pertaining to sound has been isolated and that a and b are opposed to c and d by reference to it. However, these differences are merely due to context. This can be confirmed by imagining a language such that Harris's *formal* rules always result in single and non-contradictory decisions. In such a case structure could be determined by calculation alone, and it would be superfluous to consider the sound material of the given language. All one can say is that Harris has not been able to carry out his attempt at formalizing the determination of structure to its ultimate conclusion. While the need to take the sound material into account is purely residual, it has not been eliminated. Yet formula (2) provides an accurate definition of the concept of structure in this context. The same idea can also be expressed by stating that Harris's theory is a potential classificatory model or, in other words, a system of axioms from which the classification of a system of objects can be determined by calculation. In this sense, it can be compared with models such as factorial analysis, a special case of which has been considered earlier, or the analysis of latent structure. All such models are used to classify a set of objects by reference to a theory posited *a priori*.

The true difference between this context and those described earlier is that, in the present case, formula (1), i.e.:

$$A + Str(S) \xrightarrow{\text{Calculation}} App(S)$$

cannot be applied. As this formula defines the procedure by which the validity of theory $A + Str(S)$ can be tested in the context mentioned in the previous chapter, the conclusion may be drawn that a different type of test will be required here.

In the present type of structural analysis, testing procedures are far less automatic than in previous cases and may be extremely diverse. However, they always consist in an explanatory theory of the facts pertaining to a language. When the phonologist attempts to describe the system of sound signals which constitute a language, he does so in the hope—as Harris puts it—that this description will facilitate the comparative study of language. It should also 'be important for structural linguistics and dialect geography'[1]. In other words, to test means in this case to ascertain whether the analysis is a fruitful one. This type of verification has already been mentioned and it has been suggested that it should be called *indirect*.

This is not the place to describe in detail the operations which can test the validity of a structural analysis such as this. It will suffice to mention Jakobson's work, which emphasizes the correlation between phonological description, on the one hand, and phenomena such as the beginnings of speech in children or the sequence of phoneme disappearance in those suffering from aphasia, on the other.

To sum up, the concept of 'structure' may be said to have the same meaning in the contexts of type 3, of which Harris's analysis is an example, and in those previously examined. Again 'structure' is the product of a theory imposed *a priori* upon the object analysed. In the example of Harris's research, this object is composed of the set of segments which can occur in a given language. These segments are considered as constructed on the basis of a 'code' whose existence must be assumed to account for the relationship—unambiguous at two levels—which exists between messages and sound-flows. The problem then consists in searching for the elementary units of this code.

The main difference between contexts of types 1 and 2, on

the one hand, and type 3 on the other, is that in the latter case the theory cannot be tested in the simple and *direct* way summed up by formula (1). Yet the remark made in the previous chapter ought to be repeated in this connection: while formula (1), when it applies, makes it easy to detect the falsity of a theory, it does not affect the complex mechanisms whereby a theory carries more or less conviction. In other terms: while contexts of types 1 and 2 are characterized by the fact that formula (1) can be applied to them, it does not follow that these theories can dispense with a test of *validity*—and in this they are akin to the theories of type 3.

Examples of structures of type 4

The example outlined in the previous section is characterized by the object analysed being reduced to a well-defined system. Of course, a language is made up of an infinite number of possible segments. But we have shown how this difficulty can be overcome and how Harris was able to replace this infinite material by a finite matrix in which a finite number of contexts was represented on one axis and a finite number of elementary segments on the other.

In other cases, it seems impossible both unarbitrarily to reduce to a finite system the object which one wants to analyse and at the same time to apply a testable hypothetico-deductive theory to it. As will be recalled, it has been decided to call 'type 4 structures' those which correspond to this kind of situation. Clearly, these 'structures' have a double weakness: on the one hand, they are bound to divide more or less arbitrary segments within their field; on the other, they do not provide direct criteria for their acceptance or rejection by a decision whose principles can be the subject of general agreement. In other words, one cannot verify the structural analysis by showing that consequences derived from it conform to reality, as is possible in the cases of structures belonging to types 1 and 2. However, this analysis is not carried out on natural systems, as in the examples of types 1 and 3, but on arbitrary subsystems. Yet the concept of structure has the same meaning as in the preceding contexts. Again it attempts to link an object-system with a theory explaining the interdependence of its elements.

The situation just described is characteristic of the use made of the concept of structure in sociology. In this discipline, the concept of structure is frequently associated with a demonstration of the interdependence of a system's elements; this could be qualified as *direct*. In this way, the structural description of an object in sociology often involves the demonstration that only certain combinations of criteria can be empirically observed, given a set of classificatory criteria established in advance. The *objective* of such a demonstration is thus completely identical with that of Lévi-Strauss–Bush in the analysis of kinship structures or of Miller–Chomsky in their theory of stress in the English language: it involves a demonstration of the mutual implication between the elements of a system. Similarly, the *principle* underlying the demonstration is identical: it consists again in *deducing* the interdependence of elements from a theory or set of propositions that are held *a priori* to be acceptable. The distinction is at the level of the methods employed for this demonstration. Firstly let us take a very simple example from Parsons [46]:

First let us discuss some of the problems of the modern type of 'industrial' occupational structure. Its primary characteristic is a system of universalistic–specific–affectively neutral-achievement oriented roles. There must not only be particular roles of this type but they must fit together into complex systems, both within the same organization and within the ecological complex systems linking individuals and organizations together. It is out of the question for such a system to be directly homologous with a kinship structure, so that it should be essentially a network of interlocking relationship units, as many other social structures tend to be.[2] (pp. 177–178).

Before analysing the implicit definition of the concept of structure which emerges from this text, it will help the reader to have several points of vocabulary cleared up. A simple example will suffice to show what Parsons means by 'universalistic–specific–affectively neutral–achievement oriented roles'. Let us imagine the role which in our modern industrial societies is designated by the term 'bank clerk'. In his work—in performing his 'role'—this clerk has to deal with clients. It is implicit in his role that he treat them all in the same manner: the role is thus 'universalistic'. In contrast, 'filial piety' is given to well-defined individuals (the parents of ego). Furthermore our clerk only deals with clients over very specific problems: his role is thus 'specific'. In contrast, the father–son relationship colours a whole range of exchanges implied by these two complementary roles. In addition, the contacts between the clerk and his clients are situated on 'affectively neutral' ground. Moreover one becomes a bank clerk and one does so by realizing certain aspirations. It is therefore an 'achievement oriented role'. On the other hand, certain roles like those of 'son' are ascribed.

These points of vocabulary having been clarified, the meaning of Parsons' text is obvious. He seeks to establish a contrast between certain non-industrial societies where professions or occupations are—if not determined by the position of the individual in the kinship system—at least homologous to this system, and industrial societies where professions and occupations are in most cases independent from the position of the individual in the kinship system. But Parsons goes further than this. He is not content merely to note the relationship between two facts: the 'industrial structure of occupations', on the one hand, and the absence of homology between occupational and family roles, on the other. From this relationship he deduces a proposition according to which the 'industrial structure' of occupations implies a society in which family ties are reduced to the nuclear family or 'conjugal' family:

Hence we may say with considerable confidence to those whose values lead them to prefer for kinship organization the system of medieval Europe or of Classical China to our own, that they must choose. It is possible to have either the latter type of kinship or a highly industrialized economy, but not both in the same society. (p. 178)

Later on Parsons expresses this even more forcibly: 'It can be said that the "conjugal type"...is the only kinship type which interferes relatively little with an industrial economy' (p. 178).

Leaving aside the subject of this debate—which is not our concern here—let us consider the particular meaning given to the concept of structure in this context. Parsons' reasoning is

I

more or less the following: when the individual is involved in a system of extended family relationships—as in medieval Europe or in classical China—he has to perform a great number of 'roles', which by the very definition of family roles are 'particularistic', 'diffuse' (in contrast to 'specific'), 'affective' and 'ascribed' (as opposed to 'achievement oriented'). These roles —to the extent that they have a considerable importance for individual behaviour—are incompatible with the 'industrial occupation structure'. This implies that personal aspirations are crucial for the positions attained by individuals; furthermore the occupational mobility characteristic of industrial societies and the 'achievement orientation' of occupational roles are in contradiction with the immobility implied by roles derived from family relationships, etc.

The concept of structure is thus closely associated with the idea that one cannot find any possible combination of elements in a given society. If one considers all known societies, it is clear that they can differ from one another in terms of a large number of characteristics: family organization can be of the conjugal type, as in contemporary industrial society; alternatively one can have a ramified and extended family organization, as in medieval Europe or classical China. Thus all known societies can be classified according to a certain number of criteria. However, only few combinations of such criteria appear to have existed, as Parsons himself indicates when, for example, he writes: 'From a purely taxonomic point of view any considerable prominence of kinship in social structures generally would seem highly problematic' (p. 153); or 'The actual variability...occurs within a "band" which is considerably narrower than the range of logically possible permutations and combinations' (p. 157). In other words, it can be stated that all known societies only realize a very small number of the combinations of characteristics which are logically possible. This is due to the fact that far from being unrelated to one another, these characteristics are interdependent. Thus it is not sufficient merely to observe them: it is useless merely to note the association between the economic system and the type of family organization, unless it is shown that this relationship derives from a set of theoretical propositions. If this correlation were taken for a simple empirical fact, could it not be thought that it would no longer occur in some future societies?

Here again the concept of structure is related to a well-defined objective. It involves the construction of a theory which permits the explanation or—more exactly—the deduction of the interdependence between the elements of an object-system. Multiple examples could be drawn from Parsons' work to show that the concept of structure is always related to an approach analogous in kind to that which has just been described.

The same definition of the concept of structure is frequently found in the social sciences. One can cite for example a passage of Raymond Aron drawn from a paper on the concept of 'Political Structure'.

In this research (research on structures) economics is greatly in advance of political science. It has effectively separated numerous variables or functions *which cannot but be found* in all economies of a given type. This discipline is thus in the process of identifying régimes, then concrete systems and the structures of these systems.

If one by-passes the distinctions introduced by Aron [1] between régimes, concrete systems and structures, retaining only the formal delineation of the concept of structure, it is clear that once again this is related to the idea of a *necessary* link between the characteristics of a system, as is shown by the expression in italics. The same meaning occurs in the definition given by Merton [40] to the concept of structural constraints. 'The range of variation in the items which can fulfil designated functions in a social structure is not unlimited.... The interdependence of the elements of a social structure limits the effective possibilities of change of functional alternatives...' (pp. 52–3). As Parsons had done, when he noted the impossibility of returning to a non-conjugal kinship system in an advanced industrial economy, Merton claims that unawareness of these *structural constraints* is the basic mechanism of utopian thought.

It should be underlined that all the texts just quoted emphasize the idea of *necessary* logical implications between the different variables characterizing a system. Aron speaks of variables and of functions which 'cannot but be found' in economic systems. Similarly Merton mentions the 'range of possible variation' of functional alternatives for an element, which obviously implies that certain functional equivalents are impossible. Likewise Parsons affirms that certain systems of family organization are incompatible with certain economic systems. Murdock [43] also shows in the same way (this example will be returned to in greater detail) that when residence is matrilocal or avunculocal descent is never patrilineal. Nadel [44] shows that 'A Nupe "father" may or may not have his adult sons in his labour team, and he may or may not pay their bride price when they marry'. However, of the four possible combinations of these two options only three can actually occur: that in which the son receives a dowry, but cannot be employed by the father, is ruled out.

However, if the co-occurrence of certain characteristics is considered as *necessary* or—which comes to the same thing—if the coexistence of certain elements is ruled out, this necessity will have to be demonstrated. Inversely, to demonstrate this necessity the interdependence of elements must be posited as necessary. It must be repeated that these are the basic principles underlying the use of the concept of structure in this type of context, as in others.

Indeed it seems that the methods of 'structural analysis' advanced by the authors just quoted are always related to axioms from which the interdependence between elements of a system or the impossibility of certain combinations of elements is deduced. It was to this set of axioms that Parsons devoted a tentative definition which he termed 'structural functionalism'. However, we shall provisionally leave aside the relationship between structure and function, an association which has been sufficiently criticized already. To analyse the form taken by sets of axioms in the type of context under examination, let us reconsider the arguments of Parsons: if in a given society its members occupy in most of their activities roles which are defined as 'universal', 'specific', 'affectively neutral', 'achievement oriented', this implies that the residence of such individuals is not compulsorily fixed, that they may choose the occupational activities in which they engage and that they can freely associate with other persons in the same society with whom in principle their relationships are both neutral in terms of effect and limited in kind. On the other hand, if one imagined the limiting case of a society where 'others' would all be relations, then the system of roles would be 'particularistic', 'diffuse', 'affective' and 'ascribed'. Formally the reasoning is as follows:

(1) a characteristic A implies a state of affairs $a, b, \ldots, n$;
(2) a characteristic B implies a state of affairs $a', b', \ldots m$;
(3) the states of affairs a and a', for example, are incompatible;
(4) consequently characteristic A and B cannot be present simultaneously in a society.

Obviously the degree of confidence given to such a theory essentially depends on the acceptability of the premises stated under points (1) and (2). It should be emphasized that every time reference is made to the 'structure' of a social system in the type of context referred to here, a form of reasoning can be shown which is basically identical to that just described.

It should be noted incidentally that this type of reasoning characterizes the modernistic functionalism of Merton, in contrast with the rigid functionalism of Radcliffe-Brown or Malinowski. The great difference between these two types of functionalism consists, in our view, in the form of reasoning employed by them. The supporters of absolutist functionalism claim that they can demonstrate the necessary *coexistence* of certain characteristics in a social system. On the other hand, advocates of relativistic functionalism maintain they can demonstrate that certain social characteristics are mutually *exclusive* in a system, but not that they reciprocally imply each other. The logical advantage of this relativistic functionalism is that it can rely on the type of argument outlined above, and corresponding to a sequence of clearly defined operations. By contrast, it is impossible to give formal expression to the approach of rigid functionalism. As Merton shows, it is not really possible to demonstrate that certain social elements must coexist. For example, one cannot demonstrate, as Malinowski thought he could, that a given form of society necessarily implies certain needs, which in turn imply the necessary existence of magic. It is possible to explain the existence of magic by these needs, but not to deduce the necessity of its existence from them. Yet one can show that two given characteristics would result in states of affairs which would be mutually contradictory. Thus, while the reasoning of rigid functionalism cannot be given formal expression, that of modified functionalism can. In other words, it is possible to demonstrate that two social characteristics are mutually exclusive, but not that they imply each other. If one examines the argument characteristic of the modified functionalist approach (see p. 53), it will be seen not to include the term 'function', whereas the word would have to be used in any attempted formulation of the rigid functionalist arguments.

After this digression, it can be stated that the structure of social systems as described by structural-functionalism is always the outcome of deductive reasoning applied to certain premises. Therefore the concept of structure has the same meaning in this context as in previous ones. This definition can once more be symbolized by formula (2):

$$A + App(S) \xrightarrow{\text{Calculation}} Str(S).$$

Of course the calculation which permits one to pass from $A + App(S)$ to $Str(S)$ is an elementary one in this case: it is merely a logical deduction. Verification procedures are *diffuse*, as in the type 3 contexts. Attempts are made to carry conviction by showing that the theory explains as many facts as possible.

Before considering a last example of type 4 structure—which will confirm the general character of the definition given to the concept of structure in this book—we shall sum up the comments on the concept of 'verification' which are scattered throughout this text.

The concept of verification

As has already been made clear, the thesis upheld here is that, in the context of operative definitions, the concept of structure has a simple meaning which may be summed up by saying that a structure is always the product of an *a priori* theory intended to explain an object-system as a system. Such a definition may seem disappointing or commonplace. Yet we fail to see what other definition of the concept of structure could be provided, and are deeply reluctant to uphold any *realist* stand which would consist in postulating the existence—in the world of things—of 'structures' awaiting discovery. On the other hand, we fail to see in structuralism anything other than the search for theories applicable to systems conceived as such. In other words, it is not so much a method as a class of theories whose specific character consists in attempting to account for the systematic nature of the objects with which they deal.

Consequently, the feeling of homonymy that the concept of structure gives rise to does not spring from a confusion occurring at the level of this concept—which is in fact clear and unambiguous—but results from the *quality* of the theories that are inseparable from 'structural analysis'. Moreover—as has been shown by our distinction between the four types of contexts—this quality largely depends on the intrinsic characteristics of the object analysed.

Can one doubt that to deal with a set of *well-defined* and easily observable systems—as do Lévi-Strauss or Bush in their analysis of kinship rules—is easier than to attempt—as do Max Weber or Parsons—an analysis of the consistency between the economic system and the value-system which characterize a society? Alternatively let us consider the linguistician who attempts a theory of stress in English: this is undoubtedly a difficult task and is unlikely to be completed for some while. But that is not the point. What matters is that the linguistician is—by the very nature of his object and of his objective—in a *quasi-experimental* situation. His task consists at the outset in considering a limited number of segments which are well-defined systems in themselves and whose description reduces to a statement of few characteristics. He then attempts to formulate a theory which enables him to deduce the facts of stress that characterize the segments studied. Having done so, he can—by an approach similar to the verification procedure used in the experimental sciences—select other segments which will falsify or corroborate his theory and enable him to either amend or expand it.

The sociologist endeavouring to show the *consistency* of the institutions of a global society is obviously in far less favourable a position. Hence he will produce a theory far less easy to test. This fact will result in the unfounded impression that the 'structural analysis' of the linguistician has nothing in common with that of the sociologist and that it is a verbal abuse to apply the term 'structure' to both situations.

We have already discussed somewhat inconclusively the *quality* of theories associated with structural analysis. Our thesis should now be summarized.

No one would deny that a theory is a hypothetico–deductive system or that it requires verification. But while the first proposition is unambiguous, the second raises the question of how to define *verification*.

Several references have already been made to the standpoint adopted by Popper on this issue [45]. He asserts that the concept of verification, being obscure and impossible to formalize, should be replaced by that of *falsification*. Indeed there are cases in which it can be unambiguously decided that a theory is false: it suffices to show that some consequences of the theory are disproved by observation. By contrast, one fails to see how a theory could be proved true, unless the impossibility of falsifying it is equated with its verification. Popper suggests that theories constructed in a way which makes it possible to falsify them should alone be considered *scientific*. Whether such theories are false or not is immaterial; all that matters is whether they are susceptible of falsification. This results in a dichotomy between the two types of theory: falsifiable or scientific theories and non-falsifiable theories, sometimes called *metaphysical* by Popper.

While this view adequately covers some historical phenomena concerning the natural sciences, such as the passage from Aristotelian to Galilean physics, we doubt whether it provides a fully satisfactory interpretation of the concept of verification. To be more explicit, we feel that—apart from the fundamental distinction to be drawn between falsifiable and non-falsifiable theories—another distinction should also be made between levels of falsification. This is relevant here since —if the concept of structure were associated with theories which had necessarily to be either falsifiable or not—one could not argue that its meaning would be the same in both cases: the ambiguousness surrounding the concept of theory would affect the concept of structure.

Our earlier comments tend to show that there are many levels of falsification and that the Popperian dichotomy can only be retained at the cost of gross (though useful) over-simplification. Let us mention again, in this context, the contrast between Chomsky–Miller's phonology—a sample of which has been described—and that of Harris. The theory of stress in English propounded by the former can undoubtedly be falsified, in so far as, if it were false, it would lead to incorrect deductions about the stress on given segments. A similar direct criterion does not exist for Harris's theory. Yet it provides an explanation for a number of facts connected with the geography of dialects, diachronic change, etc. Consequently there are also some criteria of falsification in this case, although they are much more diffuse than for Chomsky–Miller's theory.

Hence it could be stated summarily that the Popperian dichotomy is based on a specific criterion, whereas a whole range of criteria may be provided for the testing of a theory. According to Popper a criterion of falsification exists when some consequences of a theory T may be tested by reference to reality. Such a criterion obviously demarcates the territory of two distinct classes of theories. Yet other classes exist too. Thus, in the case of Jakobson's phonology, the ranking of phonemes by reference to their complexity is the same as some empirical sequences, such as the order in which phonemes appear in the child. Such a fact corroborates the theory, but cannot strictly be considered as a criterion of falsification, since the theory does not allow for any statement about empirical sequences of this kind. Other distinctions may be introduced: thus let us assume two theories, T and T', both of which can be falsified and which are therefore equal in relation to Popper's criterion. If many consequences testable by reference to reality $(C_1, C_2 \ldots C_n)$ can be drawn from T, whereas T' yields only one consequence testable in this way, a greater degree of confidence will be given to T than to T' (assuming neither T nor T' has been refuted). This criterion has been mentioned earlier as the 'criterion of generality'. The criterion of comprehensiveness should also be recalled. All these criteria, and not Popper's criterion of falsification alone, make it possible to attribute various levels of validity to theories.

Without pursuing this debate on the concept of *verification* in the social sciences (a debate worthy of a whole volume in its own right), we should like to conclude with an example embodying the concept of 'levels of verification' and confirming the view that it is primarily the object analysed by a theory that determines its level of verification.

Social structure and institutional coherence

This example will consist in a brief comparison between two theories concerning the coherence of social institutions: the analysis of kinship structures in the Lévi-Strauss or Bush tradition, on the one hand, and Murdock's theory of social structure, on the other.

To sum up earlier comments on the analysis of kinship structures, let us state that:

(1) The analysed object is a set of well-defined systems (the marriage rules characteristic of each system);

(2) The theory makes it possible to construct a criterion of direct verification, since it is possible to check whether the marriage rules deduced from this theory actually correspond with the rules applied in a given society. Hence the theory has a high level of verification.

By contrast, let us examine Murdock's theory [43]. The problem envisaged is the same: to account for the consistency of social institutions. In other words, the purpose is to show how social institutions mutually imply one another or to show that a society never 'chooses' an aggregate of particular institutions, but an institutional *system*. Yet, while the objective is identical for Murdock and Lévi-Strauss, the *object* is different. Murdock does not attempt to demonstrate the consistency of marriage rules alone, but that of all institutions in archaic societies. (For this purpose, Murdock compiled systematic observations concerning 250 archaic societies. The institutions observed ranged from marriage customs—bride-price, service performed for the parents-in-law, marriage with no return—to modes of social stratification, and included rules of residence, descent, inheritance etc.).

Murdock's theory consists in positing a number of principles from which the consistency of these rules can be deduced. Ideally speaking, it is conceivable that such a theory should be formalized so that it would be possible—as in the case of Chomsky–Miller's or Lévi-Strauss–Bush's theories—to *deduce* all institutions characteristic of each society. But when examining so many societies and covering such diverse institutions, one is bound to introduce specific factors which upset the postulated coherence. Moreover, though marriage rules may be considered as a rational solution to a problem which can be formulated in explicit terms (even if it is not necessarily perceived as such), this does not apply to all institutions. It is easy to state that, for example, rules of matrilineal descent appear to be more naturally associated with a matrilocal or avunculocal type of residence. Yet it seems unlikely that the co-occurrence of such rules could be deduced, as that of marriage rules could. In the latter case, change in one rule involves a modification in the general management of the system, since it is the whole set of marriage rules considered in their interrelatedness which makes it possible to achieve a balance in the exchange of women. However, in the former case, the co-occurrence of matrilineal descent rules and patrilocal residence rules would merely result in a lack of what one might call 'simplicity' in the system. Therefore all one can say is that rule x reasonably implies rule y rather than rule y'. In addition, the validity of a rule can only be assessed in relation to the whole set of other rules. Consequently the co-occurrence of rules x and y may be appropriate in a society where rule z obtains also, but unexpected in a society which does not abide by rule z. Thus even if it could be shown that x must imply the existence of y, it would be impossible to demonstrate that x *always* implies the existence of y. This accounts for the 'verification' procedure used by Murdock being 'weaker' than the level of verification characteristic of the analysis of kinship structures. He merely ascertains that the *frequency* of co-occurrence varies—as predicted by his theory—in accordance with the rules considered.

Let us examine for example the co-occurrence of descent rules and residence rules (Table I): its frequency will be seen to vary. Thus patrilocal or matrilocal residence is associated in more than half of the cases with patrilineal descent and in less than one case in ten with matrilineal descent. In one case—almost unique in the tables provided by Murdock—a rule (matrilocal or avunculocal residence) is exclusive of another (patrilineal descent or double descent).

The meaning of these correlations will be made clearer by another example. From a set of postulates Murdock deduces the following 'theorem' (his own term): 'In the presence of non-sororal polygyny, collateral relatives outside of the polygynous family tend to be terminologically differentiated from primary relatives of the same sex and generation'.

Table I. *Relationship between residence and type of descent* (according to Murdock [43])

Residence rules	Matrilineal descent	Patrilineal	Double descent	Bilateral descent	Total
Matrilocal or avunculocal	33	0	0	31	64
Patrilocal or matrilocal	15	97	17	39	168
Patrilocal neolocal or bilocal	52	105	18	75	250

We shall not try to show how this theorem is deduced from Murdock's theory; we shall simply point out the difficulties involved in its verification. To test the proposition he puts forward, Murdock attempts to demonstrate differences in the frequency of co-occurrence. However, as will be shown in Table II, the attempt is a near-failure: if one considers the second line of the Table, one notes, for example, that—contrary to forecasts based on the theorem—the wife of the father's brother and the mother are denoted by different terms with equal frequency, whether a system of non-sororal polygyny obtains or not. In other cases, differences in frequency follow the anticipated trend, but are weak and not very meaningful.

Yet the theorem is likely to be true: the fact that it is not demonstrated by Table II is due to the very high association non-sororal polygyny with patrilocal residence and patrilineal descent. These factors—as other results show—have a counter-vailing influence on terminological differentiations. If one

Table II. *Terms denoting kin in relation to forms of marriage* (actual figures) (according to Murdock [43] (p. 144)).

Pairs of relatives	Non-sororal polygyny		Other forms of marriage	
	different terms	same term	different terms	same term
Mother's sister—Mother	53	58	48	70
Father's brother's wife—Mother	36	46	37	45
Father's brother's daughter—Sister	28	84	23	95
Mother's sister's daughter—Sister	30	78	23	90
Brother's daughter—Daughter	38	61	39	73
Wife's sister's daughter—Daughter	22	28	16	24

corrects for the influence of some of these factors by eliminating part of the sample, a new table of correlations can be drawn up in which the predictions drawn from the theorem are more fully validated. For example, in the previous table, the father's brother's wife and the mother were denoted by different terms in approximately 45 per cent of cases, whether there was a system of non-sororal polygyny or not. In the following table, the corresponding percentage is 60 in systems of non-sororal polygyny and 45 in others.

It can be argued that the reason why the *level of verification* characterizing Murdock's theory is weaker than that of the Lévi-Strauss–Bush theory should be sought in the features of

the object analysed. These determine to a large extent the
maximum level of verification at which one can aim. They are
easy to recognize: they range from the fact that the proposed
analysis is to cover the *general* coherence of social institutions—
rather than that of a specific set of rules, as in the case of kinship structures analysis—to the fact that the population of
societies studied is limited. These circumstances are unlikely to
be modified.

Table III. *Terms denoting pairs of relatives in relation to forms of marriage*
(according to Murdock [43] (p. 145)).

Pairs of relatives	Non-sororal polygyny		Other forms of marriage	
	different terms	same terms	different terms	same term
Mother's sister—Mother	25	19	34	51
Father's brother's wife—Mother	16	11	23	29
Father's brother's daughter—Sister	12	33	18	69
Mother's sister's daughter—Sister	11	22	20	68
Brother's daughter—Daughter	23	17	28	50
Wife's sister's daughter—Daughter	7	9	12	16

Yet Murdock's position is exceptionally favourable in comparison with that of Parsons, for example. It is therefore conceivable that some theories should be at a lower 'level of
verification' than Murdock's—which is in turn at a lower level
of verification than the theory of kinship structures.

It is worth noting that in the analysis of *terminological* rules
associated with kinship systems, Murdock's theory takes the
form of a *general* hypothetico–deductive system. In other words,
all the propositions formulated—and tested by reference to
tables of co-occurrence such as those quoted above—are
deduced from a single theory. One of the propositions drawn

from this general theory is that there are social *equalizers*, consisting of descent rules, forms of marriage, etc., and tending to reduce differences between certain kin-types and to favour the extension of the same terms to them. From this theory is deduced, for example, the proposition that patrilineal inheritance rules must involve the use of the same terms to denote the brother's daughter and the daughter. Similarly the theorem quoted earlier is deduced from it: 'In the presence of non-sororal polygyny, collateral relatives outside of the polygynous family tend to be terminologically differentiated from primary relatives of the same sex and generation'.

By contrast, when it is not only the consistency of the terminological system associated with kinship, but the set of rules and institutions characterizing archaic societies which is analysed, the theory takes the form of several *fragmentary* theories, distinct from one another, each of which allows only for the deduction of a very limited number of theorems, or in most cases of one theorem.

In conclusion, let us take the four following theories as examples:

1. Analysis of kinship structures (Lévi-Strauss–Bush);
2. Analysis of terminological systems associated with kinship (Murdock);
3. Analysis of institutional coherence (Murdock);
4. Analysis of social systems (Parsons).

The comments made earlier can be summarized by stating that one moves from a higher to a lower level of verification when passing from theory 1 to theory 2, from theory 2 to theory 3 and from theory 3 to theory 4.

Thus Lévi-Strauss's theory, being *general* and *exact*, permits the deduction of all the marriage rules characterizing a society. On the other hand, Murdock's 'terminological' theory is still *general*, but does not allow for an *exact* deduction of the rules adopted in a given society. It can only be stated that in the presence of such and such institutions, there is a greater *probability* of encountering one rule than another in a society. The theory is at a high level of verification in spite of this 'probabilistic' character of theorems, since they all are deduced from it:

each theorem being confirmed by observation, the trust that can be placed in the theory from which they are derived can be very great. Of course, this trust is reduced when—as in the case of Murdock's theory of institutional consistency—one is confronted with a set of fragmentary theories, each of which is corroborated by a small number of theorems only (or by one theorem only). Yet an explicit, though probabilistic, criterion exists in this case and allows for the *falsification* of each fragmentary theory. Lastly, to analyse Parsons' theory of social systems—or any similar theory—is not only to deal with a set of fragmentary theories rather than with a general one, but also to be unable to define an unambiguous criterion of falsification. In such a case, complex psychological mechanics are involved in producing conviction. These differences are summarized in Table IV.

Table IV. *Classification of the four theories by reference to their levels of verification*

Criterion of falsifiability	THEORIES	
	General (single theory accounting for a large number of facts)	Fragmentary (multiple theories, accounting for a small number of facts each)
Applicable	Lévi-Strauss–Bush's theory (exact theory) Murdock's terminological theory (probabilistic theory)	Murdock's theory of institutional consistency
Not applicable		Parsons' analysis of the structure of social systems

Again we must stress the close correlation between the level of verification attained by a theory and the characteristics of its object. In the case of Lévi-Strauss, this object is well-defined and moreover constitutes a *closed* system: marriage rules can be analysed in isolation. In Murdock's 'terminological' theory, the system analysed is well-defined, but an account of linguistic practices associated with kinship systems involves the use of information virtually extending to all institutions. Indeed rules of residence or of descent—as well as many other rules—tend to result in terminological associations or dissociations. In Murdock's theory of institutional consistency, the object is *undefined*: it is impossible to exhaustively describe the institutions of a society. Yet a broad comparative basis exists in this case: it is therefore possible to draw up criteria of falsification based on statistics. Finally, in the case of an analysis such as Parsons', the object is undefined and the comparative basis very narrow. The 'theory' must almost necessarily take the form of several fragmentary theories, to which no well-defined criteria of falsification can be associated. However, this is not to say that the 'theory' is incapable of carrying conviction.

To sum up, a structure is always the theory of a system—and it is nothing else. Such theories can be located at various levels of verification, primarily dependent on the characteristics of the system considered, on the population of systems with which it can be compared and on other factors in relation to which the researcher's freedom to intervene is limited. Therefore it is likely that the concept of structure will remain homonymic for a long period yet, that is to say, that it will be associated in the social sciences with theories corresponding to widely different levels of **verification.**

Conclusion

These final remarks will be limited to a summary of the views put forward in earlier chapters.

The most obvious interest afforded by 'structuralist' methods, as applied for example to the analysis of kinship structures or to structural phonology, is that they introduce an explanatory order among incoherent phenomena. At first glance, the rules permitting or prohibiting marriage in certain societies seem incomprehensible. Why should one be allowed to marry the daughter of one's mother's brother, yet forbidden to marry the daughter of one's father's brother? Similarly, sets of grammatical rules, such as the rules of stress in the English language, seem to be aggregates of specific propositions rather than organized systems. Why should the vowel denoted by symbol *e* be swallowed in the pronunciation of 'compensation' and distinctly audible in that of 'condensation', when the two words are very similar in their phonological properties? Again if one considers the rules on kinship terms in archaic societies, these seem at first to be contingent facts which can only be recorded. How is one to explain, for example, that the daughter of one's father's sister should be called 'sister' in some cases, but not in others?

Similarly, the uses of the term 'structure' seem, at first, to be unregulated. The same word is clearly used both with different meanings and to denote the same meaning as other words. Being a collection of *homonyms*, it also belongs to a collection of *synonyms*. An even more disturbing fact is that though it is easy to establish an inductive definition of the concept of structure that meets with general agreement, this definition appears to be somewhat unsatisfactory and in any case fails to account for the success of the concept. Moreover how is one to account for the use of the same term in connection with methods as different from each other as the analysis of kinship structures, on the one hand, and Parsons' 'structural-functionalism' on the other? Finally, how is one to explain that the term *structure* should have become indispensable, if it cannot be endowed with a content very different from that of such expressions as 'essence', 'system of relationships', 'dependence of parts in relation to a whole', 'totality' and other analogous terms?

An attempt has been made here to outline an answer to these questions.

Firstly, it has been shown that one must distinguish between two types of contexts for the concept of structure: contexts of intentional definitions and contexts of operative definitions.

In the former, the role of the term 'structure' is purely terminological. It is used to formulate—to indicate—distinctions which could usually be designated by other terms: for instance the opposition between *structure* and *conjuncture* or that between *structure* and *organization*. The word 'structure' is often used in such cases because one of the contrasted terms conjures up one of the 'synonymic associations' of the concept of structure. It is not therefore surprising that the concept of structure in this type of context should be clearly defined and yet widely applicable. Paradigmatically, its definition may be reduced to a statement of its synonymic associations. Syntagmatically, it can be defined by reference to its function, which is to designate an object as *system*, to contrast two categories of objects, those which are viewed as systems and those which are viewed as aggregates, etc. Yet, while these definitions are perfectly understandable and unambiguous, it does not follow that a general inductive definition of the concept of structure in this type of context can be provided. The very nature of these definitions shows that the 'applications' of the concept of structure must vary with the environment in which it occurs. For example, it would be unreasonable to expect it to have the same content in the opposition 'structure–organization' and in the opposition 'structure–conjuncture'.

Consequently it is absurd to discuss—from a terminological point of view—what precise meaning should be given to such expressions as 'social structure', 'economic structure', etc. Provided the concepts and distinctions one attempts to introduce are clear, it does not really matter by what term they are designated. The word 'structure' is used in such cases because

—owing to its synonymic associations—it emphasizes a characteristic which one is trying to stress. Therefore discussions about defining a concept like 'social structure' either by assimilating it to the concept of organization or not, about the inclusion of inter-individual relationships within its scope, or about its limitation to group relations, etc., do not make sense and in fact derive from *realistic* metaphysical assumptions.

If one considers the other type of context, that in which an operative definition of the concept of structure is given, this concept is again synonymous with the expressions cited earlier: 'essence', 'system of relationships', 'totality irreducible to the sum of its parts', etc. However, this *synonymy* is of the same kind as that which exists between the concept 'hypothesis' and its synonymic associations. As has already been stated, a hypothesis is a provisional assertion. But the term 'hypothesis' could not have acquired an autonomous existence, as it has done in the history of science, without differing sharply from its synonyms. Indeed it implies the scientific revolution from which experimental sciences stem. To sum up, a metaphysical proposition and a hypothesis are both doubtful assertions, but the former is not a hypothesis since it cannot be falsified (or provisionally fail to be falsified).

It is claimed here that the same point can be made about the concept of structure. The structural description of an object does contrast with its phenomenal description, as essence does with *appearance*. Structural analysis does show as *coherent* the facts which appear incoherent to the outside observer. Lastly, structural description always emphasizes that the parts of an object are dependent upon the *whole*, which is the object. But if no additional statement is made, it will be difficult to understand why the term 'structure' has become so dissociated from its 'synonyms' (at least in some contexts) as to appear irreplaceable, and why it should be associated with several scientific break-throughs, as in so-called 'structural' linguistics and 'structural' anthropology.

In the light of these facts, the meaning of the concept of structure in the context of operative definitions seems almost self-evident. All that is required is to perceive, for example, what differentiates classical phonetics from structural phonology.

In the former, the object which can be designated as 'the language–considered-as-sound' is described by the phonetician rather as relief is by the geographer. In structural phonology, however, the description given results from the application of a deductive theory and is the product of a calculation or—as in the case of Harris's phonology—a 'pseudo-calculation'. The calculation is defined by reference to a number of *a priori* propositions or 'axioms'. Thus it will be posited that two sound units are *structurally* distinct if they perform a distinguishing function, and in no other case. Obviously there is no necessity to posit such a proposition which is not based on experience. Therefore it is truly *a priori*, and adopted for reasons of expediency, in the hope that it will provide for a better understanding of the facts studied. Thus when deducing from this axiom the *theorem* whereby the initial sounds of the words *kilo* and *courage* are identical in structure though different in appearance, such a statement is derived both from the objective properties of the given language and from an axiom posited by the linguistician.

Consequently the structural description of an object is defined as the whole set of *theorems* based on the application of axioms to this object. Both the axioms and the theorems constitute a theory of the object viewed as a *system*. An advantage of such a definition consists in its generality since—as has already been seen—it applies to all the widely different cases examined here and enables one to explain why the concept of structure is polysemous in this type of context.

Yet it should be mentioned that the relationships between the terms of the language referred to as 'systems theory'—namely the terms 'set of axioms', 'structural description', 'apparent characteristics', etc.—vary with the cases considered. For example, in the study of stress in the English language outlined by Chomsky and Miller, the structural description given is corroborated by the fact that the corresponding axioms allow for a correct *deduction* of stress in many segments in English (phenomenal characteristics). In the case of Harris's phonology, the 'verification' procedure is different, structural theorems being corroborated by their explanatory power in relation to an important set of linguistic facts. Generally speaking, although the concept of structure is always associated with a theory intended to show the interdependence of elements within a system, we must admit that there are several possible levels of validation for such theories. Incidentally, the level of 'verification' reached by a theory depends upon a number of criteria: Popper's criterion of falsification, the criterion of diffuse verification, the criterion of generality, the criterion of comprehensiveness, etc.

Once the correlation between the terms 'structure', 'axioms', 'verification', and 'system' has been established, and confirmed by reference to a wide range of examples, a *syntagmatic* definition of the concept of structure emerges and enables one to account for the phenomena of homonymy associated with it. Thus there is no doubt that the 'structures of kinship' in Lévi-Strauss's sense and the 'structure of social systems' in Parsons' correspond to homonymic uses of the term 'structure', at least from the vantage point of an unsophisticated observer. In attempting to analyse this feeling of homonymy, we have been able to show several types of structures—reduced to four for reasons of expediency—and to describe a number of criteria for distinguishing between them. However, it became apparent in all cases that—just as in the context of intentional definitions—the feeling of homonymy was a product of environment. In other words, while the scientific tool used seemed to us to be identical in the various examples envisaged, there is no denying that its efficacy varied with the objects to which it was applied. Yet this diversity in the 'applications' of structure generally is itself a product of context. The phenomena of stress associated with a segment of the English language or the marriage rules of a society are bound to be easy to describe in their totality, whereas a group, a society, an economic system are *undefined* wholes, irreducible to component facts. In addition, the sociologist is not able as a rule to adopt the quasi-experimental stand characteristic of linguists. Furthermore it is unavoidable that the sample of societies utilized for example by Murdock for the *verification* of his theory should have been of necessity limited, and consequently that only a limited level of verification should have been possible.

The definition given above is also useful in showing that the concept of structure, though it does not reduce to its synonymic associations, necessarily evokes them in this type of context. Indeed a structural description contrasts with a phenomenal description, as essence does with *appearance*. Moreover, being an explanatory theory, it enables one to account for facts which appear incomprehensible and to demonstrate their *consistency*. Finally, being a testable hypothetico-deductive system, it permits the *deduction* of all the elements which define the phenomenal description of an object. Within the structural theory, the set of facts comprising this description becomes a set of theorems. Hence the particular is made meaningful by its relationship with the *whole*. In short, all the synonymic associations of the concept of structure seem to be necessarily evoked by the syntagmatic definition proposed. However, the concept of *structure* is as completely distinct from these associations as a *hypothesis* is from a provisional affirmation. This two-fold statement explains the insufficient care generally taken to differentiate between the *intentional* and the *operative* definitions of the term structure.

In conclusion, does a method which could be called 'structural' or 'structuralist' exist?

The answer to this question depends on the meaning attributed to the term 'method'. If by 'structural method' or 'structuralist method' is meant the very general approach which consists in envisaging the analysed object as a whole, as a set of interdependent elements whose coherence must be shown, then such a method does exist. In fact, its existence is so obvious that it is hard to conceive of a sociologist, an economist, a linguist or an anthropologist who was not a structuralist. It is unlikely that anyone ever doubted that languages, markets, societies, and personalities were systems. By this definition, Aristotle was a structuralist since, when he introduced the concept of final cause, he clearly envisaged the living being as a system whose elements can only be understood in relation to the whole they make up. But if 'structural method' designates a set of procedures for the construction of a theory about any object, with as high a level of verification as possible and permitting one to account for the interdependence of constitutive elements—then we can say that such a method does not exist. If it did, this would mean that man would have at last found the means of constructing useful theories by complying with certain methodological rules. We have sufficiently emphasized that the structure of an object can only be outlined by a theory. Yet no one has ever formulated methodological rules for the construction of accurate and useful theories. Let us take for example important structural theories such as Harris's phonological structure, Lévi-Strauss's theory of kinship structures or Chomsky's grammatical theory. In all three cases, these theories required long gestation periods prior to their formulation. Chomsky's findings would not have been possible without Saussure and Jakobson and without the development of novel conceptual tools which enabled Chomsky to view grammar as a special mathematical structure. Lévi-Strauss's findings would not have been possible without the long tradition of thought and research on the problem of incest prohibition which predates his work. In turn he has given a strong impetus to formal research on the analysis of kinship structures in the last twenty years. Neither Lévi-Strauss nor Chomsky achieved their results by using some mysterious 'structuralist method'. More modestly, they have profited by a long research tradition to which they applied a fertile scientific imagination and a series of conceptual tools more refined than those available to their predecessors.

Thus no 'structural method' exists. There is no 'structural method' in the sense in which there is an 'experimental' method. For a theory of experiment design—tentative in Stuart Mill, complete in Fisher—does exist, though no textbook can make the researcher conduct pertinent experiments. There is no 'structural method' even in the sense in which there is a 'phenomenological' method. Without indulging in too many illusions about the interest afforded by the latter method, one must recognize that its 'inventor', Husserl, was able to describe it by formulating a few rules. Such is not the case with the 'structural method'. Therefore no such method exists. There are only specific structural theories, some of which are of great scientific importance, while others are less successful. Yet others—on which we shall not dwell—are merely gratuitous and subtle hypotheses which do not offer any likelihood of verification.

The quality of structural theories depends of course on the

imaginativeness of their authors and on earlier research, but also on the characteristics of the objects studied. Although structuralism existed in both fields, macro-sociology has probably made less progress from Montesquieu to Parsons than linguistics from Troubetskoi to Chomsky. Is this due to a mere historical accident? A more likely reason is that the questions asked by sociologists from Montesquieu to Parsons generally concern global societies, which are undefined systems and to which it is very difficult to apply comparative methods. As a result, the sociologist is reduced—because of the very nature of the object studied—to applying such methods as 'functionalism' or '*Verstehen*'. These methods alone can be applied when there is no comparative basis allowing for 'quasi-experiments'. Yet it cannot be denied that they are incapable of a high level of verification. In particular, they do not permit the construction of genuine criteria of falsification. Incidentally this is why the debates on functionalism and on *Verstehen* have never been brought to a close. Such methods, allowing for a low level of verification, are yet practically the only ones which can be applied to the analysis of global societies. Therefore it is no coincidence that structuralism should have failed to transform sociology, as it did linguistics or anthropology. Rather than to structural-functionalism, the breakthrough in modern sociology dates back to Durkheim's *Suicide*, which showed that by concentrating on well-circumscribed subjects the sociologist could adopt a quasi-experimental approach and construct theories with a high level of verification.

We are willing to acknowledge the pessimism implicit in these comments. They mean that sociology and economics—not to mention such disciplines as literary criticism[1]—cannot expect much from 'structuralism' as such. Indeed if this term has any meaning, sociology has been 'structuralist' since Montesquieu and economics at least since Walras. This may seem disappointing. But it is not absurd to believe—with those whom we have called 'magical structuralists'—that a philosophical attitude as such suffices to yield scientific success.[2] To say that an object will be envisaged as a whole, as a structure, is not enough to make the object more understandable *ipso facto*. In biology, twenty-five centuries separate Aristotle's philosophical structuralism from Sherrington's scientific structuralism and from cybernetics. It is not the alleged structuralist approach or method that has initiated the rapid progress of biology in the twentieth century. Nor was it structuralism as such that stimulated the great development of economics since Walras, but the patient and cumulative elaboration of more efficient research instruments, and the gradual perfecting of methods of observation.

Notes

Chapter 1

1. See references [2], [7], [33], [56].
2. The theory propounded by Popper [50]—which has other exponents, but of which he alone examined all the implications —is that a scientific hypothesis is a proposition whose *falsity* can be demonstrated. The advantage of replacing the concept of 'verification' by that of 'falsification' is that while it is possible to demonstrate unambiguously that a theory is false, there are no criteria to demonstrate that it is true. Indeed how is one to distinguish between a true theory and one whose falsity has not yet been demonstrated? The Popperian concept of 'falsification' is conveyed by a neologism—since in English the term 'to falsify' is not the opposite of 'to corroborate', as is shown by its use in the expression 'to falsify a document'. This comment indicates that the concept of 'verification' is naturally formed in spontaneous epistemology, but that the opposite concept is not. This is due to scientific work being summarily conceived of as a quest for the truth, whereas in practice there is no means of demonstrating the truth of a theory, only its falsity (or a provisional lack of falsity). Nothing could be more remote from spontaneous epistemology than Popper's irrefutable thesis whereby scientific work consists primarily in attempting to prove the falsity of a theory. Hence the use of the term 'falsification' in a meaning which differs from its usual one.
3. According to Popper, a *scientific theory* is one which can be falsified. In other words, it is a theory of which at least some consequences must be such that they can be unambiguously said to fit in with certain well-determined facts, or to contradict them. Thus Newton's theory of mechanics is scientific, since the inferences drawn from it can be confronted with certain facts. By contrast, Kant's theory of knowledge is non-scientific or, in Popper's words, is *metaphysical*, since no unambiguous test can be devised to falsify it. Similarly Bergson's theory of the life force is *metaphysical*, while Sherrington's theory of homeostasis is scientific. The advantage of defining a scientific theory as one which can be *falsified* rather than as one which can be *verified*

is that a simple and well-defined criterion of falsification exists, which is none other than the *modus tollens* of scholastic logic. It can be stated as follows: 'If proposition p implies proposition q and if proposition q is false, then proposition p is false'. By virtue of this criterion, one can reject a theory by demonstrating that one of its consequences is not in accordance with reality. On the other hand, it is impossible to define a finite criterion which would permit to assert the *truth* of a theory, for in order to demonstrate that a theory is true one would have to demonstrate that not one of its conclusions contradicts a single fact. Hence such a demonstration rests on a criterion which is both undefined and infinite. These considerations obviously apply only to the empirical sciences, and not to the formal sciences (logic and mathematics). In the latter, it is possible to construct finite and defined criteria of truth. Furthermore it should be stressed— and this point will be made at greater length in chapter 4— that the dichotomy posited by Popper [50] between 'scientific' and 'non-scientific' theories by reference to the criterion of falsifiability (the former always being falsifiable and the latter never) should be toned down somewhat. It accurately describes the verification procedures of the experimental sciences, but becomes inadequate in the case of the pseudo-experimental sciences, such as economics and sociology.

4. 'They [the laws] must be relative to the *physiognomy* of the country; to its climate, icy, burning or temperate; . . . to the religion of its inhabitants, to their inclinations, to their wealth, to their number, to their trade, to their customs, to their manners. Finally, they are related to each other. . . . I shall examine these relationships: together they constitute what one calls the *spirit of the laws*' (*The Spirit of the Laws*, vol. II, p. 238 of the Pléiade edition). If this quotation is compared with Murdock's book, *Social Structure*, it is found to describe the programme of this work. All the demonstrations made by Murdock consist in emphasizing correlations between institutions and between institutions and morphological elements. In brief, Murdock shows that 'the laws are interrelated', that they have relationships with *mores*, 'commerce' (i.e. the economic system), etc. Moreover, as these relationships are deduced by Murdock from a theory, they are consequently viewed as necessary relationships, rather than as mere experimental truths. Thus Murdock believes with Montesquieu that 'laws are related to each other', that they are related to customs, to 'trade' (i.e. to the economic

system, etc.). Although the demonstration is made in different ways by Montesquieu and by Murdock, the logic of their approach is the same. What Murdock calls *social structure* is exactly that which Montesquieu called the *spirit of the laws*. It goes without saying that this expression, *spirit of the laws*, although inspired by the legal vocabulary, was used by Montesquieu as a neologism: laws are necessary relationships derived from the nature of things; the spirit of the laws is what we would call the logic of these relationships, which not only Murdock, but— as will be seen in chapter 4—all sociologists designate by the term 'structure'.

Chapter 2

1. On factor analysis, see references [20], [54], [55].

2. Readers pressed for time may move on to page 27 and admit that the hypothesis outlined on p. 24 and expressed by equation $zij = ajGi + eij$ results in $^rjk = aiak$, in which ^rjk designate the coefficient of correlation between test j and test k.

3. This typology has been borrowed from Davis [11], [12].

4. To support the interpretation given here, it should be noted that contextual (Lazarsfeld) or structural (Blau) propositions represent a considerable progress in sociological survey techniques. Until recently surveys remained *atomistic* or individual: in other words, information about individuals was collected, but it was impossible to measure the impact of their social position on their attitudes and behaviour. This enabled Blumer [5] to state that surveys were not appropriate tools for sociology, since they could not grasp situations 'as wholes' or take 'social structures' into account. While this criticism could be addressed to a type of surveys, it is no longer justified in relation to contextual ones. In these, the propositions are formulated not about an individual, but about the system constituted by the individual and the social situation in which he is placed. Thus the purpose is no longer to show that individual attitudes or opinions are dependent upon biographical data or upon other opinions and attitudes, but to show the interdependence between individual states and social situation. For example, when Lipset and his collaborators [34] show that the size of workshops in the printing industry has an 'effect' upon the degree of political and unionist information possessed by the workers (the best

informed work in large workshops), and on the difference
between union officials and the rank and file with regard to
information, it is the whole situation of the worker which in a
way is analysed by the survey. It could be said that the survey
apprehends the 'structure' of the situation in which the observed
individual finds himself. It can be understood in this light that
the concept of contextual (Lazarsfeld) or structural (Blau)
propositions may be envisaged as an operational interpretation
of what is generally meant by the vague terms of 'social structure', 'structure of situations', etc.

5. On the matrix analysis of 'group structures', see references
   [3], [14], and [16].

6. See [27], [29]. In an atomistic survey, a number of individuals
   is investigated; in a contextual survey, after selecting a set of
   'milieux' (institutions, groups etc.), one observes either a sample
   or the whole individual membership. It can thus be determined
   to what extent variations in individual behaviour are due to
   variations in environmental characteristics.

7. 'It is known that each distinctive unit may be defined in two
   different ways. On the one hand, by reference to the contexts
   in which it is found: e.g. the old Greek /s/ may be defined as the
   non syllabic phoneme which appears as initial before another
   non syllabic phoneme and as final; this is a syntagmatic
   definition. On the other hand, by noting the phonic or semantic
   features which distinguish this unit from others of the same level:
   the French /b/ is sonorous as compared with /p/, oral as compared with /m/, bilabial as compared with /v/ and so on; this
   is a paradigmatic definition which emphasizes that which
   opposes the units which can be found in the same contexts'
   (Martinet [37], p. 124). Let us remember from this text that a
   paradigmatic definition is based on substance or content and a
   syntagmatic definition on relationships with the context.

8. See note 5.

9. Obviously a concept such as 'life force' is but a new term to
   convey the old concept of final cause.

Chapter 3

1. Readers will have understood that there is no contradiction
   between the fact that 'intentional' definitions of the concept of

structure are always in the form of definitions by distinction and the impossibility for the concept of structure to be inductively defined in the context of intentional definitions. Indeed, a careful distinction must be drawn between two view-points; that of the specialist, who—whether he is a sociologist, a psychologist or an economist—attempts to define the concept of structure in a given context, on the one hand; and, on the other, that of the methodologist, who analyses the *meaning* of these definitions. The former is bound to use inductive definitions; but the latter, if he seeks a definition of this kind by 'comparing and abstracting common elements' from the definitions suggested by the sociologist, the psychologist and the economist, can only record that the concept is *polysemous*.

2. See references [21], [22], [37].

3. A few comments on the problem of 'verification' will be made in chapter 4.

4. The inverted commas convey the relative inappositeness of the word 'choice'. Tests are not selected like a sample of individuals from among a population. It is a fiction to put the selection of a battery of tests in the same category as a choice from among a population of tests. Obviously this population is not defined.

5. In the whole of this text, the concept of 'structural description' and the axioms formulated in this connection are presented in a *simplified* and consequently a deliberately inaccurate way.

6. By *calculation* is meant a series of operations which can be performed mechanically, i.e. such that their sequence and nature are unambiguously defined in advance. For a rigorous definition of this concept, see Martin [36], p. 16.

7. In common practice 'structure' is sometimes identified with what is designated here by '$Str(S)$' and sometimes with the 'theory' $A + Str(S)$. In the expression 'the structures of kinship', the term structure is identified with $A + Str(S)$. The concept of 'structural description', used by Chomsky–Miller, identifies the concept of 'structure' with $Str(S)$. In econometrics, a structure is the whole of $A + Str(S)$, but references are also made to the 'structural parameters' of a model. In the latter case, the following definitions are made: 'model' $= A$, 'structural parameters' $= Str(S)$, 'structure' $= A + Str(S)$.

8. A later publication will deal with the structural analysis of myths as it is carried out, for example, in *Le Cru et le Cuit*. The

concept of structure can be shown to have the same meaning in this context as in others. This demonstration has not been made in the present book, because it would have been too lengthy. The logical schemes used by Lévi-Strauss in *Le Cru et le Cuit* are far more complex than those of the examples presented here. They require a painstaking exegesis which, had it been attempted, might have diverted the reader's attention from the main topic—the concept of structure in the human sciences—to the very different theme of the structural analysis of myths.

9. This feeling of arbitrariness is naturally the obverse of the inability of classical theories to account for these rules.

10. All the philosophical problems which arise in connection with the concept of 'theory' arise therefore also in connection with the concept of 'structure'. We do not believe that the scientific theories of physics imply a specific theory of knowledge. This is also true of the 'structuralist' theories propounded in the human sciences. It may be said either that structural analysis leads to the essence of things or that it missess essentials. Neither in physics nor in poetry does anything enable one to demonstrate that the physicist understands the *physis* better than the poet, or that the opposite is true.

11. The model presented here hardly differs at all from those used in econometrics. See, for example, Tinbergen [56].

12. This means that no table can be interpreted without reference to the other tables. On these points see reference [6].

13. The causal formulation used here is merely convenient: it makes it easy to express the hypotheses which, when formalized, determine the 'structure' of the process. See reference [6].

14. On the details of this procedure, see [6], chapter 7.

15. It should be noted that in French there is a difference (without counterpart in English) between *structural* and *structurel*. Although these two French adjectives are often interchangeable, they embody a distinction: *structurel* usually corresponds to the noun *structure*, and *structural* to *structuralisme* (being therefore often an attenuated version of *structuraliste*). When Barthes claims to be *homme structural* (structural man), he means that he subscribes to the *Weltanschauung* which he seeks to discover in structuralism. Linguistics is *structural* in so far as it relies on a 'structuralist' approach. But the parameters of an econometric model are

structurels, since they describe the structure of a set of data. Similarly, one will refer to the description of a spoken segment as being *structurelle*. However, it would be possible to talk of group analysis as either *structurale* or *structurelle*. The latter is more usual, since the stress is less on the 'structuralist' approach used than on the object of the analysis: to determine the structural properties of the groups. But it is more common to refer to the analysis of a literary text as *structurale* in order to emphasize the 'structuralist' approach adopted.

Chapter 4

1. Harris [21], p. 3.
2. See also, on the concept of structure in Parsons, the useful introduction by F. Bourricaud to the French edition of *Elements of a Sociology of Action* [47].

Conclusion

1. Structuralism 'applied' to literary criticism by authors like Barthes or Goldmann would deserve an analysis which cannot be provided here. Careful examination of their work would no doubt show that structuralism in literary criticism is associated with the same scientific *intentions* as in other fields. In other words, it would show that the *wish* of the literary critic is to construct a theory of his object from which the fundamental characteristics of this object can be deduced. Direct evidence of this intention could easily be found. In a recent text ('Introduction à l'analyse structurale des récits' *Communications*, 1966, 8, 1–27, p. 2), Barthes writes of the structural analysis of narratives: 'It is necessarily condemned to proceed by deduction; it must first devise a hypothetical descriptive model (called a "theory" by American linguists) and then gradually descend from this model to the specific instances which both participate in it and deviate from it. . . .' Such a text shows clearly that Barthes attributes to the concept of 'structural analysis' a meaning similar to that of, for example, Murdock or Chomsky. Yet no one can doubt that the 'hypothetical models' mentioned by Barthes are often so hypothetical in practice as to defy any attempt at verification or falsification. In other words, they are not real hypotheses, if it is accepted that the concept of hypothesis implies those of verification or falsification. This had been demonstrated by Raymond Picard [50] in connection with

the 'hypothetical models' by which Barthes attempts to explain Racine's tragedies. These models are propositions, often inventive, but not susceptible of corroboration or disproval. Consequently, structuralism in such cases is completely redirected away from its true meaning. It acquires a *latent function*, which consists in endowing arbitrary statements with the credit earned by 'structuralist methods'—whose success in linguistics or anthropology cannot be denied. This dual nature of structural analysis applied to literature (in our present state of knowledge) has been recognized by Barthes himself who, in the text already quoted, states that this analysis coincides with the formulation of deductive theories, but admits that it is scarcely possible to construct such theories about the objects he examines. This results in strange texts—such as the one cited in the Foreword—where Barthes makes structuralism into a sort of *habitus* through which 'structural man' allegedly accedes to 'something which would remain invisible, or if one prefers incomprehensible, in the natural object'. There is no more reference to deduction, but rather a statement about the mysterious authority pertaining to 'structural man'.

Therefore the short history of the alliance between literary criticism and structuralism is not unlike that of its relationship with sociology. In all disciplines, efforts are being made to replace by deductive methods that which sociologists termed *Verstehen* and literary critics the 'intelligence' of texts. This progress has been accomplished in some spheres. The passage from Malinowski's rigid functionalism to Merton's qualified functionalism and to that of Lévi-Strauss and Murdock shows this to be the case. But it is striking that this progress should have transformed only a limited number of disciplines; in others—such as macro-sociology—the effects and achievements of structuralism are still very limited and localized. This is due to the extreme variability of the logical properties possessed by the objects which these disciplines study. Of course, a truly structuralist sociology or literary criticism may exist in fifty years time. Methodological innovations may permit the deductive analysis of global societies or of complex speeches. This is not only possible, but probable. But it is unreasonable to believe that some mysterious *structural methods* already exist whose instant application would propel forward such disciplines as macro-sociology or literary criticism and would achieve intelligibility.

Bibliography

[1] ARON, RAYMOND, 'Note sur la structure en science politique', in *Sens et usages du terme structure*, ed. R. Bastide, The Hague, Mouton, 1962, pp. 108–13.

[2] BASTIDE, ROGER (ed.), *Sens et usages du terme structure.* The Hague, Mouton, 1962.

[3] BERGE, CLAUDE, *La Théorie des graphes et ses applications*, Paris, Dunod, 1958.

[4] BLAU, PETER M., 'Formal organizations: dimensions of analysis', *The American Journal of Sociology*, 63, 1957, pp. 58–69.

[5] BLUMER, HERBERT, 'Public opinion and public opinion polling', *American Sociological Review*, 13, 1948, pp. 542–54.

[6] BOUDON, RAYMOND, *L'analyse mathématique des faits sociaux*, Paris, Plon, 1967.

[7] CENTRE INTERNATIONAL DE SYNTHÈSE, *Notion de structure et structure de la connaissance*, Paris, Albin Michel, 1957.

[8] CHOMSKY, NOAM, 'Explanatory models in linguistics', in *Logic, Methodology and Philosophy of Science*, ed. E. Nagel, P. Suppes and A. Tarski, Stanford, Cal., Stanford University Press, 1962, pp. 528–50.

[9] CHOMSKY, NOAM and MILLER, GEORGE A., 'Introduction to the formal analysis of natural languages', in *Handbook of Mathematical Psychology* ed., R. Duncan Luce, Robert R. Bush and E. Galanter, New York, Wiley, 1963, vol. 2, pp. 269–321.

[10] COLIN, CHERRY, *On human communication*, New York, Wiley, 1957.

[11] DAVIS, JAMES A., *Great Brooks and Small Groups*, Glencoe, Ill., The Free Press, 1961.

[12] DAVIS, JAMES A., SPAETH, JOE L. and HUSON, CAROLYN, 'A technique for analyzing the effects of group composition', *American Sociological Review*, 26, 1961, pp. 215–25.

[13] EVANS-PRITCHARD, *The Nuer*, 1940. Quoted by NADEL, S. F., *op. cit.*

[14] FESTINGER, LEON, SCHACHTER, STANLEY, and BACK, KURT, 'Matrix analysis of group structures', in *The Language of Social Research*, ed. P. Lazarsfeld and M. Rosenberg, Glencoe, Ill., The Free Press, 1955, pp. 358–67. French translation in *Le Vocabulaire des sciences sociales*, ed. R. Boudon and P. Lazarsfeld, Paris, Mouton, 1965, pp. 240–46.

[15] FLAMENT, CLAUDE, 'L'étude mathématique des structures psycho-sociales', *Année psychologique*, 58, 1958, pp. 119–31.

[16] FLAMENT, CLAUDE, *Théorie des graphes et structure sociale*, Paris, Mouton et Gauthier-Villars, 1965.

[17] GOLDSTEIN, KURT, *La Structure de l'organisme*, Paris, Gallimard, 1951.

[18] GRANGER, GILLES-GASTON, *Pensée formelle et sciences de l'homme*, Paris, Aubier, 1960.

[19] GURVITCH, GEORGES, 'Le concept de structure sociale', *Cahiers internationaux de sociologie*, 19, 1955, pp. 3–44.

[20] HARMAN, HARRY H., *Modern Factor Analysis*, Chicago, University of Chicago Press, 1960.

[21] HARRIS, ZELLIG S., *Methods in Structural Linguistics*, Chicago, University of Chicago Press, 1951.

[22] JAKOBSON, ROMAN, *Essais de linguistique générale*, Paris, Les Éditions de Minuit, 1963.

[23] KATONA, GEORGE, *Psychological Analysis of Economic Behavior*, New York–London, MacGraw-Hill, 1951.

[24] KEMENY, JOHN G., SNELL, J. LAURIE and THOMPSON, GERALD L., *Introduction to Finite Mathematics*, Englewood-Cliffs, N. J., Prentice-Hall, 1956.

[25] KROEBER, A. L., *Anthropology*, New York, quoted by LÉVI-STRAUSS, *Anthropologie structurale*, op. cit.

[26] LAZARSFELD, PAUL F., 'Intervention' in *Sens et usages du terme structure*, ed. R. Bastide, The Hague, Mouton, 1962, p. 160.

[27] LAZARSFELD, PAUL, 'Problems in methodology', in R. Merton, L. Broom and L. S. Cottrell, *Sociology Today*, New York, Basic Books, 1959. Ed. quoted: New York, Harper, 1965, pp. 39–80.

[28] LAZARSFELD, PAUL, BERELSON, BERNARD and GAUDET, HAZEL, *The People's Choice*, New York, Columbia University Press, 1948.

[29] LAZARSFELD, PAUL and MENZEL, HERBERT, 'On the relation between individual and collective properties', in *Complex Organizations*, ed. A. Etzioni, New York, Holt, Rinehart and Winston, 1961, pp. 422–40.

[30] LÉVI-STRAUSS, CLAUDE, 'La notion de structure en sociologie', in *Anthropologie structurale*, Paris, Plon, 1958, p. 303–51.

[31] LÉVI-STRAUSS, CLAUDE, *Les Structures élémentaires de la parenté*, Paris, Presses Universitaires de France, 1949.

[32] LÉVI-STRAUSS, CLAUDE, *Le Cru et le Cuit*, Paris, Plon, 1964.

[33] LÉVY, EMILE, *Analyse structurale et méthodologie économique*, Paris, Génin, 1960.

[34] LIPSET, S. M. et al., 'The psychology of voting', in *Handbook of Social Psychology*, ed. G. LINDZEY, Reading, Mass., 1954, pp. 1124–1176.

[35] MANNHEIM, KARL, *Ideology and Utopia*, Routledge and Kegan Paul, 1954. (First German edition: 1929.)

[36] MARTIN, ROGER, *Logique contemporaine et formalisation*, Paris, Presses Universitaires de France, 1964.

[37] MARTINET, ANDRÉ, 'Structural linguistics', in *Anthropology Today*, ed. A. L. Kroeber, Chicago, University of Chicago Press, 1953, pp. 574–86.

[38] MARTINET, ANDRÉ, *La Linguistique synchronique*, Paris, Presses Universitaires de France, 1953, (3rd edn).

[39] MERLEAU-PONTY, MAURICE, *La Structure du comportement*, Paris, Presses Universitaires de France, 1953 (3rd edn).

[40] MERTON, ROBERT, *Social Theory and Social Structure*, Glencoe. Ill., The Free Press, 1957 (rev edn).

[41] MILLER, GEORGE A., 'Models for language', in *Mathématiques et sciences sociales*, Compte rendu des travaux des stages de Menthon-Saint-Bernard (1–27 July 1960) et de Gösing (3–27 July 1961). Paris, Mouton, 1965, p. 283–340.

[42] MOULOUD, NOËL, 'Réflexions sur le problème des structures', *Revue philosophique*, 55, 1965, pp. 55–70.

[43] MURDOCK, GEORGE P., *Social Structure*, Glencoe, Ill., The Free Press, 1965 (1st edn 1949).

[44] NADEL, S. F., *The Theory of Social Structure*, London, Cohen and West, 1957.

[45] PAGES, ROBERT, 'Le vocable "structure" et la psychologie sociale', in *Sens et usages du terme structure*, ed. R. Bastide, The Hague, Mouton, 1962, pp. 89–99.

[46] PARSONS, TALCOTT, *The Social System*, Glencoe, Ill., The Free Press, 1951.

[47] PARSONS, TALCOTT, *Eléments pour une sociologie de l'action*, introduced and translated by F. Bourricaud, Paris, Plon, 1955.

[48] PIAGET, JEAN, *Éléments d'épistémologie génétique*, Paris, Presses Universitaires de France, t. II, *Logique et équilibre*.

[49] PIAGET, JEAN, 'Problémes généraux de la recherche inter-disciplinaire et mécanismes communs', Paris, UNESCO (roneo).

[50] PICARD, RAYMOND, *Nouvelle Critique ou nouvelle imposture*, Paris, Pauvert, 1966.

[51] POPPER, KARL, *Logik der Forschung*, Vienna, Springer, 1935. Enlarged English edition: *The logic of scientific discovery*, New York, Hutchinson, 1959.

[52] RADCLIFFE-BROWN, A. R., *Structure and Function in Primitive Societies*, Glencoe, Ill., The Free Press, 1952.

[53] RICŒUR, PAUL, 'Structure et herméneutique', *Esprit*, novembre 1963, pp. 596–627.

[54] SPEARMAN, CHARLES, 'General intelligence, objectively determined and measured', *American Journal of Psychology*, 15, 1904, pp. 201–93.

[55] THURSTONE, LOUIS, *Multiple Factor Analysis*, Chicago, The University of Chicago Press, 1947.

[56] TINBERGEN, JAN, *Econometrics*, London, Allen and Unwin, 1950.

[57] VIET, JEAN, *Les Méthodes structuralistes dans les sciences sociales*, Paris and The Hague, Mouton, 1965.

Name Index

Aristotle, 13, 14, 51, 124, 141
Aron, R., 11, 119

Barthes, R., 148–50
Bergson, H., 143
Bernard, C., 14
Blau, P. M., 29–33, 36–8, 54, 55, 145–6
Blumer, H., 29, 145
Bourricaud, F., 149
Bush, R. R., 79, 87, 116, 123, 126, 127, 129, 131, 132

Cannon, W. B., 13
Chomsky, N., 11, 21, 64–6, 70, 72, 73, 75–8, 79, 85, 87, 99, 102, 116, 125, 126, 127, 137, 140, 141, 147, 149
Cournot, A., 14

Davis, J. A., 33, 37, 145
Democritus, 102
Descartes, R., 1, 9
Durkheim, E., 29–30, 36, 38, 141

Evans-Pritchard, E. E., 43

Fisher, R. A., 140
Flament, C., 2, 8, 53, 54

Galileo, 13, 124

Goldmann, L., 149
Goldstein, K., 19–21, 27, 37
Gurvitch, G., 17–19, 27–8, 36–8, 39, 41, 42, 44
Guttman, L., 49–50

Harris, Z. S., 11, 60, 104, 106–8, 110, 112–14, 115, 125, 137, 140
Hugo, V., 12
Husserl, E., 140

Jakobson, R., 11, 59, 60, 77, 125, 140

Kant, I., 3, 143
Katona, G., 53, 54
Kemeny, J. G., 81
Kroeber, A. L., 11, 12, 41, 42, 50

Lazarsfeld, P. F., 29, 37–8, 39, 45, 47, 54, 145–6
Leibniz, G. W., 1, 9
Lévi-Strauss, C., 3–5, 8, 9, 11–12, 14, 17, 21, 28, 46, 55, 63, 116, 123, 126, 127, 129, 131, 132, 138, 140, 148, 150
Lévy, E., 7
Lipset, S. M., 145

Malinowski, B., 121, 150

Mannheim, K., 43
Martin, R., 147
Martinet, A., 6, 104, 105, 146
Menzel, H., 29, 37–8, 39, 45, 54
Merleau-Ponty, M., 19–21, 27–8, 37, 39
Merton, R. K., 119–21, 150
Mill, J. S., 140
Miller, G. A., 11, 64–6, 70, 72, 73, 75–8, 79, 85, 87, 116, 125, 127, 137, 147
Molière, 8
Montesquieu, C. de, 15, 62, 141, 144–5
Murdock, G. P., 52, 55, 120, 126–32, 138, 144–5, 149, 150

Nadel, S. F., 11, 12, 120
Newton, I., 143

Pagès, R., 5
Pareto, V., 14
Parsons, T., 5, 11, 52, 55, 63, 116–20, 123, 130, 131, 132, 133, 138, 141, 149

Piaget, J., 2, 8, 17
Picard, R., 149
Popper, K., 13, 124–6, 138, 143–4

Racine, J., 150
Radcliffe-Brown, A., 43, 121
Ricoeur, P., 88
Ruger, 20

Saussure, E. de, 14, 140
Sherrington, C. S., 13, 142, 143
Snell, J. L., 81
Spearman, C., 22–4, 27, 28, 49–50, 52, 54, 55, 58, 62

Thompson, G. L., 81
Tinbergen, J., 93, 148
Troubetzkoi, N., 60, 141

Viet, J., 7

Walras, L., 14, 141, 142
Weber, M., 123
Weil, A., 79
White, H., 79

Subject Index

Analysis (factorial), 52, 54, 62, 99, 113, 145
Anthropology, 3, 14, 99, 100, 136, 139
Associationism, 19
Axiom (concept of), 9–10; or proposition, 9, 27, 58, 72, 81–3, 137

Cause (concept of), 10
Code, coding, 76, 104, 114
Comprehensiveness (of a theory), 74–5
Conjuncture, 40–1, 44, 45, 135
Conscience (collective), 36
Criticism (literary), 141, 149–50

Determinism, 36

Economics, 5, 14, 40, 55, 99–100, 119–20, 139, 141, 148, 155
  economic structure, 44, 135
  economic system, 14, 40, 100, 119, 120, 123, 138
Effects, additive, 37; collective, 31–7; compositional, 37; contextual, 37; individual, 31–6; interaction, 37; structural, 30, 32–8, 39, 55–6

Elections (presidential in U.S.A. in 1940), 90–8
Essence, 42, 46, 48, 49, 89, 101, 135, 136, 139, 148
Experiment design, 140

Falsification, 11, 60, 124–5, 132–3, 143–4
Function (of the concept of structure), 7–9, 16–17, 134–6
  functional alternatives, 120
Functionalism, 121–2

Generality (of a theory), 73–5
Grammar, classical, 80
  grammatical theory, 140
  transformation cycles, 70–1
Groups, authoritarian or democratic, 42
  organized, 41
  non-structured, 17, 18, 39
  real, 18
  structured, 17, 18, 31–8, 39, 55–6

Homeostasis, 13
Hypothesis (concept of), 8–9, 11, 12, 48–9, 83, 136, 139, 143

Isomorphic concept, 6

Kariera (society), 80, 83–5
Kinship (structures), 11, 12, 14, 17, 28, 52, 61, 63, 79–89, 116, 117, 118, 123, 126, 130, 131, 134, 138–40

Lesion (visual field), 20

Marriage (rules), 57, 61, 62, 79–89, 100–1, 119, 126–30, 134, 138
Mathematics, Blau's linear, 29–35
  Spearman's linear, 23–8
  mathematical analysis, 13
  mathematical model, 28, 52, 79, 91–2
Method(s), experimental, 139–40
  inductive, 8
  structuralist, 63, 139–140

Occupation, 'industrial' structures of occupations, 116–18
Organization, 19, 41–7, 135, 136

Phenomenology (phenomenological method), 25
Phonemes, 5, 45, 47, 105, 106, 107, 109–12, 114, 145
  paradigmatic definition, 106, 146
  syntagmatic definition, 106, 114, 146
Phonetics (classical), 4, 5, 7, 104, 136
Phonology, Harris 'rules', 110–13
  structural 4, 5, 7, 46, 55, 60, 77, 103–5, 125, 134, 137
Proof (concept of), 9

Role, 116–18, 120, 121

Stress (in the English language), 61, 64–76, 99, 114–15, 116, 123, 125, 134, 137
Structure, collection of homonyms, 5, 7, 11, 57–65, 99–101, 123, 133, 134, 138
  definition by construction, 54
  by distinction, 54, 147
  constitutive, 46–7
  Flament's, 2, 53–4
  inductive, 3–13, 46, 134–5, 147
  intentional—chapter II, 53, 54, 135, 136, 139, 147
  Katona's, 53–4
  operative, 16, 21–9, 48, chap. III, chap. IV, 135, 136, 139
  paradigm, 46–7
  Paiget's, 2, 17
  syntagmatic, 138 (see also constitutive)
  Guttman's ordinal structure, 49
  structure of behaviour, 19–20, 39–40
  structure of the organism, 19–21
  personality structure, 62, 64
  structure of a process, 91–8
  structure of political systems, 11
  social structure, 5, 40–4, 47–8, 52, 55, 126, 135–6, 145
  Spearman's factorial structure, 22–9, 49–50, 58
  structural functionalism, 120, 134–5
  synonyms associated with the concept of structure, 1–2, 6, 7, 8, 11, 13, 14, 19, 20, 23, 28, 37, 39, 40, 42, 43, 45–6, 57–8, 78, 89, 134–6, 138

Surveys, atomistic, 45, 48, 146
contextual or structural, 30,
37, 45, 47, 90, 146
Suicide, and religion, 29–36
System, artificial, 89
authoritarian, 42
systematic character of an
object, object-system, 28–9,
37, 42–5, 46–51, 54, 55,
56–8, 60–1, 63, 101, 102,
119, 123, 135
hypothetico-deductive testable, 28, 58, 59, 60, 62, 115,
138
hypothetico-deductive in-
directly testable, 28, 58,
59, 60, 62, 115, 138
hypothetico-deductive un-
testable, 60, 62–4
of relationships, 2–3, 5, 6, 7,
8, 10, 36, 37, 38, 42, 43,
45–8, 53, 90, 135, 136
social, 40, 41, 42, 45, 52, 62,
131, 132, 138
undefined, 60, 62, 89, 100,
101
well-defined, 61–3, 79, 89,
100, 115, 123, 126

Tarau (society), 61, 81, 86–7

Variable, analytical, 45
collective, 34–5
contextual, 48
dependent, 31
explanatory, 35
independent, 31
individual, 34–6
structural, 45, 46, 47, 54
Verification (concept of), 9,
122–6, 138
Voting behaviour, 90–9